Francis Hastings Doyle

The Return of the Guards

And Other Poems

Francis Hastings Doyle

The Return of the Guards
And Other Poems

ISBN/EAN: 9783744713498

Printed in Europe, USA, Canada, Australia, Japan

Cover: Foto ©Thomas Meinert / pixelio.de

More available books at **www.hansebooks.com**

THE
RETURN OF THE GUARDS
AND OTHER POEMS

THE

RETURN OF THE GUARDS

AND OTHER POEMS

BY

SIR FRANCIS HASTINGS DOYLE

LATE FELLOW OF ALL SOULS COLLEGE, OXFORD

London
MACMILLAN AND CO.
1883

Printed by R. & R. CLARK, *Edinburgh*.

PREFACE.

THESE Poems of mine were given to the world, in their latest form, shortly before I was elected to the Poetry Professorship at Oxford—that is a good many years ago. They have long been quite out of print; but, as they had answered their purpose, I let them be. For some time past, however, I have been told by different persons, in various ways, that a new edition of them would be welcomed by that subdivision of the human race which interests itself in Poetry at present. I have, therefore, made arrangements for their republication.

Since I ceased to be Poetry Professor, I have not had much to do with literary pursuits. The circumstances of my life have left me without ambition, and without much interest in any thing but my family, my friends, and my country, of whose future I try not to despair.

However, I have written a poem now and then. And of these more recent poems some, having been added to the older compositions, will be found in the new volume. On the other hand, a few of those previously given to the world, though they may be later in point of date than many of the verses now collected, do not re-appear.

"The Two Destinies," though by no means one of my first efforts, was published whilst I was yet young, and hopeful of a more decided success as a poet than has fallen to my lot; when I looked at it again, after a long interval, the other day, it pleased me well enough, and I therefore determined on reproducing it at the end of the book, as it also has long been entirely out of print.

CONTENTS.

	PAGE
DEDICATORY STANZAS	xi
THE RETURN OF THE GUARDS	1
TO THE MEMORY OF CAPTAIN ARTHUR WATKIN WILLIAMS WYNN	6
THE DONCASTER ST. LEGER	11
THE OLD CAVALIER	20
THE VISION OF ER, THE PAMPHYLIAN	24
THE VETERANS OF THE GRAND ARMY MEETING NAPOLEON'S ASHES FROM ST. HELENA	42
THE SPANISH MOTHER	47
GYTHIA	54
HOW LORD NAIRN WAS SAVED	83
MEHRAB KHAN	87
THE RED THREAD OF HONOUR	90
THE PRIVATE OF THE BUFFS	95
DEMOSTHENES	97
LADY AGNES	105
TO TWO SISTER BRIDES	116
THE POETASTER'S PLEA	121

CONTENTS.

	PAGE
The Hyperborean Maiden	127
The Athenian Battle-Hymn at Marathon	129
Robin Hood's Bay	133
The Unobtrusive Christian	146
Stanzas written in Dejection	148
The Night and the Day	150
The Mother and Daughter	159
In Memoriam	165
Sonnet to Helen	168
To an Old Coat	169
The Horse of the Desert	171
The Mameluke Charge	175
Lines on the Sale of the Black Arab	177
Lines on a White Cyclamen brought from Jerusalem	181
Rizpah, Daughter of Aiah	183
The Duke's Funeral	185
Napoleon the Idol	194
The Epicurean	202
The Platonist	204
The Fusiliers' Dog	206
The Sirens	209
The Old Age of Sophocles	216
From the Coliseum at Rome to my Wife at Nice	219
From Heine	222
Stanzas suggested by the Above	222

CONTENTS.

	PAGE
CAIUS MANLIUS CAPITOLINUS	224
BALACLAVA	234
LINES TO HELEN	237
I SAW HER LAST	239
THE SAVING OF THE COLOURS	242
THE FOSTER BROTHER	247
THE LOSS OF THE BIRKENHEAD	256
VERSES WRITTEN FOR MUSIC	259
SEQUEL TO THE ABOVE	261
SHORT ANALYSIS OF THE "PLURALITY OF WORLDS"	263
AN EPITAPH IN COBHAM CHURCHYARD TURNED INTO VERSE	264
EPITAPH ON A FAVOURITE DOG	264
ODE FOR MUSIC	265
THE QUICK MARCH OF THE FOURTEENTH REGIMENT	272
IPHITION	277
DARKNESS AND LIGHT	280
SECRET AFFINITIES	283
THE FOUNTAIN	286
AT SEA	288
A FAREWELL	292
THE SECOND OLYMPIAN ODE OF PINDAR	293
THE FIRST CHORUS IN THE BACCHANALS	300
THE TWO DESTINIES	306

DEDICATORY STANZAS.

TO MY WIFE.

On tides fast-ebbing borne along,
    I pause, and look in silence back,
Through all the varying shapes which throng
    Life's faint and fading track.

By turns I sigh, by turns I smile,
    Wise now to see, when Hope is gone,
How Nature, with unending guile,
    Lures youth for ever on.

Where are the glittering visions fled,
    Which seemed like firm-set earth to me?
The dawn of glory, burning red
    As sunrise o'er the sea?

Such dreams before young eyes abound,
    If lost to me, they are not dead,
But twine their golden falsehood round
    Some other boyish head:

That course not idly Nature runs,
    Nor weaves those airy spells in vain;
So has she found her favourite sons,
    Again, and yet again.

Searching, and sifting men from men,
    Thus works she, till her work be done,
But flings away waste thousands, when
    She chooseth out—the One.

Yet, ruthless though she be, and cold,
    This common earth may well be trod,
Not hers, to grant or to withhold,
    The better gifts of God.

Time teaches us that oft One Higher,
    Unasked, a happier lot bestows,
Than if each blighted dream-desire
    Had blossomed as the rose;

That if bright hope, in life's decline,
    No more, like Spring, the fancy stirs,
Soft memory's Autumn lights may shine
    On richer bloom than hers.

Dearest and best, if chequered years
    Might well be wished for once agen,
If we have shed no hopeless tears,
    Nor envied other men;

DEDICATORY STANZAS.

If by thy presence, which at first
    Flashed through each morning vapour thin,
To light more radiant has been nursed
    The spirit life within;

If, thrilling us with impulse sweet,
    Day after day, from rooms above,
The pattering tread of tiny feet
    Has filled our souls with love;

What matters it, compared with this,
    That wealth, or power, or glory fails?
There grows that amaranth flower of bliss,
    Near which the laurel pales.

Such amaranth flower has been mine own,
    Through thee, for many a golden year,
Take Thou, for they are thine alone,
    These earthlier blossoms here.

October 1866.

THE RETURN OF THE GUARDS.

July 9, 1856.

YES, they return—but who return?
   The many or the few?
Clothed with a name, in vain the same,
   Face after face is new.

We know how beat the drum to muster,
   We heard the cheers of late,
As that red storm, in haste to form,
   Burst through each barrack gate.

The first proud mass of English manhood.
   A very sea of life,
With strength untold, was Eastward rolled,—
   How ebbs it back from strife?

The steps that scaled the Heights of Alma
   Wake but faint echoes here;
The flags we sent come back, though rent,
   For other hands to rear.

Through shouts, that hail the shattered banner,
    Home from proud onsets led,
Through the glad roar, which greets once more
    Each bronzed and bearded head;

Hushed voices, from the earth beneath us,
    Thrill on the summer air,
And claim a part of England's heart
    For those who are not there.

Not only these have marched from battle
    Into the realms of peace—
A home attained—a haven gained,
    Where wars and tumults cease.

Whilst thick on Alma's blood-stained river
    The war-smoke lingered still,
A long, low beat of unseen feet
    Rose from her shrouded hill;

By a swift change, to music, nobler
    Than e'er was heard by man,
From those red banks, the gathered ranks
    That other march began.

On, on, through wild and wondrous regions,
    Echoed their iron tread,
Whilst voices old before them rolled—
    " Make way for Alma's dead."

Like mighty winds before them ever,
    Those ancient voices rolled;
Swept from their track, huge bars run back,
    And giant gates unfold;

Till, to the inmost home of heroes
    They led that hero line,
Where with a flame no years can tame
    The stars of honour shine.

As forward stepped each fearless soldier,
    So stately, firm, and tall,
Wide, wide outflung, grim plaudits rung
    On through that endless hall.

Next, upon gloomy phantom chargers,
    The self-devoted came,
Who rushed to die, without reply,
    For duty, not for fame.

Then, from their place of ancient glory,
    All sheathed in shining brass,
Three hundred men, of the Grecian glen,
    Marched down to see them pass.

And the long-silent flutes of Sparta
    Poured haughty welcome forth,
Stern hymns to crown, with just renown,
    Her brethren of the North.

Yet louder at the solemn portal,
   The trumpet floats and waits;
And still more wide, in living pride,
   Fly back the golden gates.

And those from Inkerman swarm onwards,
   Who made the dark fight good—
One man to nine, till their thin line
   Lay, where at first it stood.

But though cheered high by mailèd millions
   Their steps were faint and slow,
In each proud face the eye might trace
   A sign of coming woe.

A coming woe which deepened ever,
   As down that darkening road,
Our bravest tossed to plague and frost,
   In streams of ruin flowed.

All through that dim despairing winter,
   Too noble to complain,
Bands hunger-worn, in raiment torn,
   Came, not by foemen slain.

And patient, from the sullen trenches
   Crowds sunk, by toil and cold—
Then murmurs slow, like thunders low,
   Wailed through the brave of old.

THE RETURN OF THE GUARDS.

Wrath glided o'er the Hall of Heroes,
    Anguish, and shame, and scorn,
As clouds that drift, breathe darkness swift
    O'er seas of shining corn.

Wrath glided o'er the Hall of Heroes,
    And veiled it like a pall,
Whilst all felt fear, lest they should hear
    The Lion-banner fall.

And if unstained that ancient banner
    Keep yet its place of pride,
Let none forget how vast the debt
    We owe to those who died.

Let none forget THE OTHERS, marching
    With steps we feel no more,
Whose bodies sleep, by that grim deep
    Which shakes the Euxine shore.

TO THE MEMORY

OF

CAPTAIN ARTHUR WATKIN WILLIAMS WYNN,

OF THE 23D ROYAL WELSH FUSILIERS.

Who fell gloriously at Alma, 20th September 1854.

"There lay Colonel Chester, and four of his gallant officers, with their faces to the sky."—*Morning Paper.*
"He had gone right up to the gun."—*Private Letter.*

WHEN, from grim Alma's blood-stain'd height,
   There came the sound of woe,
And in thy first and latest fight
   That noble head was low;
As those who loved and trembled, knew
That all their darkest fears were true;
Each fond heart, clinging to the dead,
Felt fiery thirst within it burn—
A restless throbbing hope to learn
How in those hours, each gloomy thread
   Of waning life was spun.

DEATH AT ALMA.

And yearnings from thine English home
Bounded across the ocean foam :—
　"Where did ye find my son?"
The answer, from that fatal ground,
Came pealing, with a trumpet sound,
　"Close to the Russian gun,
"With many a gallant friend around him,
"In one proud death—'twas thus we found him.

"He lay, where dense the war-cloud hung,
"Where corpse on corpse was thickest flung—
"Just as a British soldier should;
　"The sword he drew,
　"Still pointing true
"To where the boldest foemen stood.
"His look, though soft, was calm and high;
"His face was gazing on the sky,
"As if he said, 'Man cannot die,
　"'Though all below be done.'
"Thus was it that we saw him lie,
　"Beneath the Russian gun."

Right up the hill our columns sped,
No hurrying in their earnest tread;
The iron thunder broke in storms,
　Again, and yet again—
On their firm ranks, and stately forms,
　It did but break in vain;

Though all untrained by war to bear
    The battle's deadly brunt,
The ancient heart of Wales was there,
    Still rushing to the front.
Their blood flowed fast along those steeps,
    But the proud goal was won,
And the moon shone on silent heaps,
    Beyond the Russian gun.
For there, with friends he loved around him,
Among the foremost dead—they found him.

Oh, there are bitter tears for thee,
Young sleeper by the Eastern sea,
Grief that thy glory cannot tame;
    It will not cease to ache,
And anguish beyond any name,
    In hearts that fain would break:
Still, thy brave bearing on that day
Lends to those mourners strength to say,
    "Thy will, O God, be done.
"We bow before Thy living throne,
"And thank Thee for the mercy shown,
"Even when Thy summons dread was thrown
    "Forth from the Russian gun."
No agony that gasps for breath
Lengthened his hopeless hours of death,
No quenchless longing woke in vain
For those he ne'er could see again.

DEATH AT ALMA.

By noble thoughts and hopes befriended,
By Honour to the last attended,
His haughty step the hill ascended;
At once—his hand and brain reposed,
At once—his dauntless life was closed;
One mystic whirl of mighty change—
One sea-like rush of blackness strange—
And all the roaring tumult dim
Was cold, and dark, and still, for him,
Pain cannot rack, or fever parch,
   Now that his course is run,
And ended that majestic march
   Up to the Russian gun;
For there, with friends he loved around him,
Serene as sleep—they sought and found him.

And still for ever fresh and young,
   His honoured memory shall shine,
A light that never sets, among
   The trophies of his ancient line.
Yea, though the sword may seem to kill,
Each noble name is living still,
   A ray of Glory's sun.
And many a child, remembering well
How by sad Alma's stream he fell,
His tale with boyish pride shall tell,
   "I bear the name of one
"Who, in that first great fight of ours
"Against the tyrant's servile powers,

"Upon the red Crimean sod
"Went down for liberty and God,
  "Close to the Russian gun;
"For there, with friends he loved around him,
"Among the free-born dead—they found him."

October 1854.

THE DONCASTER ST. LEGER.

This poem is intended to illustrate the spirit of Yorkshire racing, now unhappily, or happily, as the case may be, on the decline. The perfect acquaintance of every peasant on the ground with the pedigrees, performances, and characters of the horses engaged—his genuine interest in the result—and the mixture of hatred and contempt which he used to feel for the Newmarket favourites, who came down to carry off his great national prize, must be well known to any one who forty years ago crossed the Trent in August or September:—altogether it constituted a peculiar modification of English feeling, which I thought deserved to be recorded; and in default of a more accomplished Pindar, I have here endeavoured to do so.

THE sun is bright, the sky is clear,
    Above the crowded course,
As the mighty moment draweth near
    Whose issue shows *the horse.*

The fairest of the land are here
To watch the struggle of the year,
The dew of beauty and of mirth,
Lies on the living flowers of earth,
And blushing cheek and kindling eye
Lend brightness to the sun on high:
And every corner of the north
Has poured her hardy yeomen forth;

The dweller by the glistening rills
That sound among the Craven hills;
The stalwart husbandman who holds
His plough upon the eastern wolds;
The sallow shrivelled artisan,
Twisted below the height of man,
Whose limbs and life have mouldered down,
Within some foul and clouded town,
Are gathered thickly on the lea,
Or streaming from far homes to see
If Yorkshire keeps her old renown;
Or if the dreaded Derby horse
Can sweep in triumph o'er her course;
With the same look in every face,
The same keen feeling, they retrace
The legends of each ancient race:
Recalling Reveller in his pride,
Or Blacklock of the mighty stride,
Or listening to some gray-haired sage
Full of the dignity of age;
How Hambletonian beat of yore
Such rivals as are seen no more;
How his old father loved to tell
Of that long struggle—ended well,
When, strong of heart, the Wentworth Bay [1]
From staggering Herod strode away:

---

[1] Bay Malton. King Herod, the champion of Newmarket in the famous race alluded to above, broke a blood vessel in the crisis of the contest.

How Yorkshire racers, swift as they,
Would leave this southern horse half way,
But that the creatures of to-day
Are cast in quite a different mould
From what he recollects of old.
Clear peals the bell; at that known sound,
Like bees, the people cluster round;
On either side upstarting then,
One close dark wall of breathless men,
Far down as eye can stretch, is seen
Along yon vivid strip of green,
Where keenly watched by countless eyes,
'Mid hopes, and fears, and prophecies,
Now fast, now slow, now here, now there,
With hearts of fire, and limbs of air,
Snorting and prancing—sidling by
With arching neck, and glancing eye,
In every shape of strength and grace,
The horses gather for the race;
Soothed for a moment all, they stand
Together, like a sculptured band,
Each quivering eyelid flutters thick,
Each face is flushed, each heart beats quick;
And all around dim murmurs pass,
Like low winds moaning on the grass.
Again—the thrilling signal sound—
And off at once, with one long bound,
Into the speed of thought they leap,
Like a proud ship rushing to the deep.

A start! a start! they're off, by heaven,
Like a single horse, though twenty-seven,
And 'mid the flash of silks we scan
A Yorkshire jacket in the van;
   Hurrah! for the bold bay mare!

I'll pawn my soul her place is there
 Unheaded to the last,
For a thousand pounds, she wins unpast—
   Hurrah! for the matchless mare!

A hundred yards have glided by,
 And they settle to the race,
More keen becomes each straining eye,
 More terrible the pace.
Unbroken yet o'er the gravel road
Like maddening waves the troop has flowed,
 But the speed begins to tell;
And Yorkshire sees, with eye of fear,
The Southron stealing from the rear.
 Ay! mark his action well!
Behind he is, but what repose!
How steadily and clean he goes!
What latent speed his limbs disclose!
What power in every stride he shows!
They see, they feel, from man to man
The shivering thrill of terror ran,
And every soul instinctive knew
It lay between the mighty two.

The world without, the sky above,
   Have glided from their straining eyes—
Future and past, and hate and love,
   The life that wanes, the friend that dies,
E'en grim remorse, who sits behind
Each thought and motion of the mind,
These now are nothing, Time and Space
Lie in the rushing of the race;
As with keen shouts of hope and fear
They watch it in its wild career.
Still far ahead of the glittering throng,
Dashes the eager mare along,
And round the turn, and past the hill,
Slides up the Derby winner still.
The twenty-five that lay between
Are blotted from the stirring scene,
And the wild cries which rang so loud,
Sink by degrees throughout the crowd,
To one deep humming, like the tremulous roar
Of seas remote along a northern shore.

In distance dwindling to the eye
Right opposite the stand they lie,
   And scarcely seem to stir;
Though an Arab scheich his wives would give
For a single steed, that with them could live
   Three hundred yards, without the spur.
But though so indistinct and small,
You hardly see them move at all,

There are not wanting signs, which show
Defeat is busy as they go.
Look how the mass, which rushed away
As full of spirit as the day,
So close compacted for a while,
Is lengthening into single file.
Now inch by inch it breaks, and wide
And spreading gaps the line divide.
As forward still, and far away
Undulates on the tired array
Gay colours, momently less bright,
Fade flickering on the gazer's sight,
Till keenest eyes can scarcely trace
The homeward ripple of the race.
Care sits on every lip and brow.
"Who leads? who fails? how goes it now?"
One shooting spark of life intense,
One throb of refluent suspense,
And a far rainbow-coloured light
Trembles again upon the sight.
Look to yon turn! Already there
Gleams the pink and black of the fiery mare,
And through *that*, which was but now a gap,
Creeps on the terrible white cap.
Half-strangled in each throat, a shout
Wrung from their fevered spirits out,
Booms through the crowd like muffled drums,
"His jockey moves on him. He comes!"
Then momently like gusts, you heard,

"He's sixth—he's fifth—he's fourth—he's third;"
And on, like some glancing meteor-flame,
The stride of the Derby winner came.

And during all that anxious time,
(Sneer as it suits you at my rhyme)
The earnestness became sublime;
Common and trite as is the scene,
At once so thrilling, and so mean,
To him who strives his heart to scan,
And feels the brotherhood of man,
That needs *must* be a mighty minute,
When a crowd has but one soul within it.
As some bright ship with every sail
Obedient to the urging gale,
Darts by vext hulls, which side by side,
Dismasted on the raging tide,
Are struggling onward, wild and wide,
Thus, through the reeling field he flew,
And near, and yet more near he drew;
Each leap seems longer than the last,
Now—now—the second horse is past,
And the keen rider of the mare,
With haggard looks of feverish care,
Hangs forward on the speechless air,
By steady stillness nursing in
The remnant of her speed to win.
One other bound—one more—'tis done;
Right up to her the horse has run,

And head to head, and stride for stride,
Newmarket's hope, and Yorkshire's pride,
Like horses harnessed side by side,
    Are struggling to the goal.
Ride! gallant son of Ebor, ride!
For the dear honour of the north,
Stretch every bursting sinew forth,
    Put out thy inmost soul,—
And with knee, and thigh, and tightened rein,
Lift in the mare by might and main;
The feelings of the people reach,
What lies beyond the springs of speech,
So that there rises up no sound
From the wide human life around;
One spirit flashes from each eye,
One impulse lifts each heart throat-high,
One short and panting silence broods,
O'er the wildly-working multitudes,
As on the struggling coursers press,
So deep the eager silentness,
That underneath their feet the turf
Seems shaken, like the eddying surf
    When it tastes the rushing gale,
And the singing fall of the heavy whips,
Which tear the flesh away in strips,
    As the tempest tears the sail,
On the throbbing heart and quivering ear,
Strike vividly distinct, and near.
But mark what an arrowy rush is there,

"He's beat! he's beat!"—by heaven, the mare!
Just on the post, her spirit rare,
When Hope herself might well despair;
When Time had not a breath to spare;
With bird-like dash shoots clean away,
And by half a length has gained the day.
Then how to life that silence wakes!
Ten thousand hats thrown up on high
Send darkness to the echoing sky,
And like the crash of hill-pent lakes,
Out-bursting from their deepest fountains,
Among the rent and reeling mountains,
At once, from thirty thousand throats
   Rushes the Yorkshire roar,
And the name of their northern winner floats
   A league from the course, and more.

THE OLD CAVALIER.

"For our martyred Charles I pawned my plate,
    For his son I spent my all,
That a churl might dine, and drink my wine,
    And preach in my father's hall:
That father died on Marston Moor,
    My son on Worcester plain;
But the king he turned his back on me,
    When he got his own again.

"The other day, there came, God wot!
    A solemn, pompous ass,
Who begged to know if I did not go
    To the sacrifice of Mass:
I told him fairly to his face,
    That in the field of fight,
I had shouted loud for Church and King,
    When he would have run outright.

THE OLD CAVALIER.

"He talked of the Man of Babylon
    With his rosaries and copes,
As if a Roundhead wasn't worse
    Than half a hundred Popes.
I don't know what the people mean,
    With their horror and affright;
All Papists that I ever knew,
    Fought stoutly for the right.

"I now am poor and lonely,
    This cloak is worn and old,
But yet it warms my loyal heart,
    Through sleet, and rain, and cold,
When I call to mind the Cavaliers,
    Bold Rupert at their head,
Bursting through blood and fire, with cries
    That might have waked the dead.

"Then spur and sword, was the battle word,
    And we made their helmets ring,
Howling, like madmen, all the while,
    For God, and for the King.
And though they snuffled psalms, to give
    The Rebel-dogs their due,
When the roaring-shot poured close and hot,
    They were stalwart men and true.

"On the fatal field of Naseby,
    Where Rupert lost the day,
By hanging on the flying crowd
    Like a lion on his prey,
I stood and fought it out, until,
    In spite of plate and steel,
The blood that left my veins that day,
    Flowed up above my heel.

"And certainly, it made those quail
    Who never quailed before,
To look upon the awful front
    Which Cromwell's horsemen wore.
I felt that every hope was gone,
    When I saw their squadrons form,
And gather for the final charge,
    Like the coming of the storm.

"Oh! where was Rupert in that hour
    Of danger, toil, and strife?
It would have been to all brave men,
    Worth a hundred years of life,
To have seen that black and gloomy force,
    As it poured down in line,
Met midway by the Royal horse,
    And Rupert of the Rhine.

"All this is over now, and I
    Must travel to the tomb,
Though the king I served has got his own,
    In poverty and gloom.
Well, well, I served him for himself,
    So I must not now complain,
But I often wish that I had died
    With my son on Worcester plain."

THE VISION OF ER, THE PAMPHYLIAN.

This Poem is founded on the well-known legend with which Plato concludes his great treatise on the Republic. I have written some introductory stanzas, and have ventured to throw back the time of its supposed occurrence to an era more decidedly mythic and pre-historical than Plato seems to have contemplated. With these exceptions, I have followed his details as closely as I could.

I.

STILL in her virgin prime, the earth was young;
 Through fair Pamphylia's myrtle-shadowed glades
No helmet gleamed, no threatening trumpet rung,
 To break the pure hymn of her bright-haired maids;
Unkindled yet the War-God's altar flame,
And his red planet glared without a name.

II.

Year after year, self-sown the shining corn
 Sprang freshly from the unexhausted soil;
Year after year, from terraced hills were borne
 Rivers of wine and fragrant floods of oil—
Whilst milk-white herds, unchecked, along each rill,
Knee-deep in perfumed grasses, roamed at will.

III.

Behind, to chain the storm-wind's angry burst,
   Rose mountain forests, walling out the North;
Against their peaks, by silver ocean nursed,
   Mild rain-clouds broke, and poured their treasure forth,
To cheer the land with streams, which, foaming free,
Down from bright cliffs danced headlong to the sea.

IV.

A happy people, crowned with golden flowers,
   Serenely beautiful, and pure, and true,
Like sinless children, spend the fleeting hours
   In love and joy and pleasures ever new—
Nor to that life of theirs, with roses sown,
Is man-like work, or God-like thought unknown.

V.

For theirs the ancient blood, the wondrous birth
   One under many names, whose sons we trace
Through many lands, the salt of the wide earth;
   Unsevered then with them, each gift and grace,
Now through a thousand channels scattered wide,
Were sparkling in the fountain, side by side.

VI.

Rich is that blood with Hellas, yet to be,
   Homers, still silent, through those pulses beat,
In their fresh veins, the Teuton bold and free,

The loyal Mede, the subtle Indian, meet—
Slavonic charm, Law-reverencing Rome,
And the Celt's depth of passion for his home.

VII.

Thus strong with powers and instincts half divine,
    The world's great morning filled them with its fire;
Beneath their hands the quarry and the mine
    Grew into shapes of beauty—the dumb lyre
Found sudden soul and breath and utterance given,
And thrilled in rapture to the smiling heaven.

VIII.

Though no dull Cadmus yet had taught his kind,
    Like frost-nipped bees, about dead signs, to cling;
The Poet's song round his own heart was twined,
    As blossoms clothe a fruit-tree in the spring,
And passed through time, along the lips of men,
For memory was a living spirit then.

IX.

In the nymph-haunted grove, on festal days,
    The Bard aroused keen ranks of listening youth;
Wove each wild legend into magic lays,
    And veiled with beauty all the gaps of truth;
Or taught his few how mystic wisdom ran,
Through seers unnumbered, from primæval man.

X.

Thus the glad æon glideth swift along,
  With choral dance, and grand heroic game,
With wealth unblamed, high thought, and noble song,
  For ever shining, like a star, the same—
Whilst gracious kings, the seed of Gods above,
Unfeared, though reverenced, rule the land in love.

XI.

Till some far chief, Lord of a ruthless will,
  Fused myriads into one grim lava-flood;
Made glory mean the brute desire to kill;
  And marched on power, through blighting steams of blood.
Like winter wolves, grim septs, o'er wastes unknown,
Flocked at the scent of gore, around that throne.

XII.

And though through him no temples upward sprung,
  No stately docks or havens hummed with trade;
Though in his tent no tuneful harps were strung,
  Nor bard, nor sage, in shining robes arrayed,
Sat at the King's right hand—his gloomy mind
Was strong to marshal and to rule mankind.

XIII.

With brain all fire, whilst all his heart was ice,
  Pitiless, though not cruel, on he went,

To honour dead, yet unenslaved by vice,
   No passion mastered, and no scruple bent—
Himself his god, he deem'd e'en fate his own,
And gazed on stars, that burned for him alone.

XIV.

As the moon guides the sea, his aspect swayed
   The fierce, yet feeble nature of the crowd;
Half-love, half-awe, they trembled and obeyed;
   Round that slight form each mail-clad giant bowed:
Watched, as he fell, that face through eye-balls dim,
And bought, with life, one frozen smile from him.

XV.

The brain gave insight, and its stedfast ken,
   No pulse of human sympathy could shake:
Clear thoughts do much for iron tempers, when
   We are but tools to use, or toys to break;
O'er trampled hearts, through many a blazing town
Thus marched the first great conqueror to renown.

XVI.

And on, and on, and on, the deluge streams,
   Swelled by uprooted nations in its course,
Until that sacred race from happy dreams
   Started, to hear the tramp of Scythian horse—
And dusky clans, white-toothed, and lithe, and wild,
In ape-like swarms through every glen defiled.

XVII.

But not in vain had lions felt their steel,
   Not idly bled the panther in his den,
The imperial people was not made to kneel,
   But mustered her unconquerable men—
Whilst high above those jabberings harsh and grim,
Rolled the proud thunder of their Aryan hymn.

XVIII.

The records of that battle, let them rest,
   Its dead were dust, ere writer shaped a reed,
Enough, that Er, their bravest and their best,
   Lay cold beneath his white Cilician steed:
Mere loss to them, to him that change hath brought
But ampler insight, and diviner thought.

XIX.

Freed from the burthen and the cloud, he soars
   To join the souls which gather from afar;
Following some unknown guide to unknown shores,
   Beyond the sun and every golden star—
All called that morn from light, and hope, and breath,
Gently or roughly, by the voice of Death.

XX.

From every land, in ordered companies,
   The unending phantoms came, matrons and maids,

Children, with wonder in their placid eyes,
   And clothed in seeming steel, heroic shades:
But still supreme o'er all the breeds of man,
   The Aryan chiefs were marshalled in the van.

XXI.

Then swiftly gliding through empyrean air,
   They reach at length a wondrous Spirit Home.
Twin caves stretch down into that darkness, where
   Hell's iron roots are lashed with fiery foam,
Whilst right above them set, like gems, on high,
Twin gaps in heaven burn through the purple sky.

XXII.

There sit the silent rulers of the dead
   Between those glooms and glories; at their nod
About the good inspiring gleams are shed,
   And voices whisper from the soul of God,
But round each wicked sprite, a deepening cloud
Gathers and blackens like a sable shroud.

XXIII.

Yet as Er drifted past, his Judge to meet,
   On him nor gleam, nor penal shadow fell;
But a voice thundered from the shining seat,
   "What thou beholdest here remember well.
"Fate bids thee learn, then to thy kind rehearse,
"All that upholds this wondrous universe.

XXIV.

"No more from evil can ye claim release;
  "No longer live the life of summer flowers—
"For the old times of purity and peace
  "Are gone for ever with their golden hours;
"Slow through the world, your hearts at length to gain,
"Hath ate the canker and hath spread the stain.

XXV.

"Rouse then thy keenest insight to discern
  "What the earth's orbit is, and still must be;
"How for themselves their lot the wicked earn,
  "And what the purpose of eternity,
"That though like others into suffering brought,
"Ye may not die unguided and untaught."

XXVI.

Thus warned, in silence the Pamphylian Lord
  Stood like a star; across his thoughtful face,
Like cloud on cloud, in rushing visions poured.
  The Story of the Past, then melts in space,
And left the ghosts, still radiant, or in gloom,
Between those four abysses, waiting doom.

XXVII.

Straight through one gem-like gap, uprising slow,
  The spirits of the just were lost in light,

Whilst its bright sister lent to earth below
    A stream of blissful aspects, all in white—
Souls, from their place of glory called afresh,
To wear once more the fetters of the flesh.

XXVIII.

Meanwhile the left-hand cave of night devours
    Each clouded spectre cursed of Fate's decree,
As some wide water swalloweth falling showers,
    Its horror closed above them, like a sea—
But on the right, from Hell a ghastly train
Rolled upward through the lurid cleft amain.

XXIX.

Like corpses haunted, stealthily they came,
    With pale Fear living in their eyes alone—
Then clasped their fleshless hands, which bonds of flame
    Had charred to dust around each mouldering bone—
Whilst hope once more, in each chilled heart, arose,
Like a stray moonbeam upon mountain snows.

XXX.

With the fierce swoop of locusts on ripe grain,
    Swarmed all these Terrors at the appointed place,
Yet writhing from a thousand years of pain,
    They met the sons of heaven there face to face;
Whose calm still lustre, broken at the sight,
Thrilled into trembling gleams of roughened light.

XXXI.

So, when in spring the gay south-west awakes,
    And rapid gusts now hide, now clear, the sun,
Round each green branch a fitful glimmering shakes,
    And through the lawns and flowery thickets run,
(Tossed out of shadow into splendour brief),
The silver shivers of the under-leaf.

XXXII.

But as they joined each other, Hell and Heaven
    Brightened or faded to the hues of earth—
They stand once more, rewarded or forgiven,
    Upon the threshold of a second birth—
Once more their hearts with human thoughts were rife,
And human memory started into life.

XXXIII.

Then flowed affection back, and keen desire
    To learn each secret of the solemn past.
And the good told, how ever mounting higher,
    From sphere to sphere, each nobler than the last,
They near the central throne of God above,
    And bask undazzled in His smiles of love.

XXXIV.

But the forgiven ones, with shuddering awe,
    Recount their travel through Hell's angry deep;

A hundred dreary years, for such the law,
   Through trackless thorns and scathing fire they creep,
Then that each crime may tenfold penance meet,
Ten times that dismal circuit they repeat.

XXXV.

Yea for the worst, the traitor lurking nigh,
   Like some foul spider couched in poisonous twine,
Or brutal kings, who faith and truth defy,
   To drink a people's tears and blood like wine.
These, by the fixed intelligence of Fate,
Woes heavier still, yea, ceaseless pangs await.

XXXVI.

Said one, "Why comes not Ardys back, who died
   "Some thousand years ago, a king of men?"
But the pale strugglers from beneath replied,
   "Ardys the great ariseth not again—
"Too foul the sins he made high heaven endure,
"For God to pardon, or for pain to cure.

XXXVII.

"Just where the black is touched with ashen gray,
   "He wrestled upward through the lessening gloom,
"But sudden forms of fire beset the way,
   "And yon grim Hell-gap thundered out his doom—
"For him, dragged down to adamantine chains—
"No end, no respite, and no hope, remains.

XXXVIII.

"Yea, and for others, as for him, that sound,
　"With earthquake roar broke forth, and at the sign,
"Those living demon-flames enclosed them round,
　"And hurled their victims home to wrath divine;
"So that we shivered by, unnerved, aghast,
"Scarce hoping for a silence, as we passed."

XXXIX.

Thus the souls communed in those mystic hours,
　And Er sat listening to the tales they told,
In meadows gay with fountains and with flowers,
　Seven days they rest, or wander, uncontrolled—
But on the eighth uprise the heavenly guides,
And in their wake the spirit phalanx glides.

XL.

Three days they march, and on the fourth behold,
　Stretched through the sky, a column of keen light,
To which the rainbow's flush is pale and cold,
　Through this, in complicated windings bright,
The mighty knots, and giant links, which bind
The heavens and earth together, pass entwined.

XLI.

And at the light's edge, deftly joined thereto—
　Like a ship's helm, with chains which none may sever,

The distaff of Necessity works true,
   And wheels the rolling universe for ever—
Rim over rim, each rising inwards higher,
In eight concentric orbs of living fire.

XLII.

The outer movement is of stars which burn,
   And whirl the heavens with one undying force.
On paths reverse,—within the planets turn,
   Opposed, but yet harmonious in their course ;
Thus, from of old, self-poised and uncreate,
Round spins that Distaff on the knees of Fate.

XLIII.

On each a Siren stands sublimely still,
   Whilst from each eddying circle, soft is thrown
One single note, which swells uprising, till
   All mix in mighty music round God's throne ;
And on three seats, with spaces wide between,
Sat solemn, three crowned virgins, each a queen—

XLIV.

Of old Necessity the seed sublime—
   Clotho, and Atropos, and Lachesis,
To whom lies bare, throughout the coils of time,
   Eternity's ineffable abyss—
Clad in white robes, with utterance calm and strong,
They chant an echo to that siren-song.

XLV.

Stern Lachesis still summons back the Past;
   To Atropos alone, divinely wise,
Is given the clouded Future to forecast—
   Pale Clotho of things Present, as they rise,
Sings ever; whilst the mingling voices run,
Present and Past and Future seem but one.

XLVI.

To that high Temple, Fate's unchanging home,
   Float up, like following waves, the destined dead—
On through the solemn lights which flood the dome,
   Unheard, of bloodless millions falls the tread—
Whilst some one whispers, "Here is Heaven's decree,
   "The maiden Lachesis now speaks through me.

XLVII.

"Ye short-lived souls, once more the years return,
   "Once more for you the dreams of earth begin,
"And a new race beneath the sun shall learn
   "How man is born to sorrow and to sin,
"And yet this hour is yours. If used aright,
   "Your joys may yet be pure, your burthens light.

XLVIII.

"We grant to each his chance,—reproach us not
   "If lust or avarice lure your hearts astray,

"For know, once fixed the self-selected lot,
  "Each in the prison of his choice shall stay;
"Lives, bright at first, in heaviest gloom may close,
"Rich wines hold poison, asps infect the rose.

XLIX.

"Whilst like thick clouds, all sun and warmth behind,
  "Fates black without with inward light may glow,
"So let the first be wary, lest he find
  "Frail splendours wane to darkness, death, and woe,
"Nor let the last lose hope, since God may prize
"Much on this earth, which blinded men despise."

L.

The shades draw near obedient to that call,
  And as they gaze in eager wondering dumb,
Lives from her lap like snow-flakes whirling fall,
  Rich with the destiny of worlds to come,
And lots are swift assigned to choose the same,
"Then yours alone," she cried, "the praise or blame."

LI.

On rush the spirits, in their ranks, to share,
  Those myriad fortunes, hiding all the plain;
Princedom or serfship, happy love, despair,
  With every form of glory or of gain;
Tempted, by power, the first, in stooping down,
Forgot the ills which wait upon a crown.

LII.

Nor till the coming years could change no more,
   Marked he the end, how, pressed by hostile Fate,
He was foredoomed to drink his children's gore;
   Then angry Horror grasped his heart too late;
Reviling Heaven in vain, he stood forlorn,
And cursed the fate impending, yet unborn.

LIII.

But he was hurried on, and others came
   Who, as their bitter memory backward ran,
Full of fierce wrath, and anguish, hate, or shame,
   Renounced the form, and scorned the hopes of man
To lurk a lion in the woods, or scream
A lonely eagle o'er the mountain stream.

LIV.

Those who had died in youth, an eager throng,
   Snatched at tumultuous pleasure mixed with pain—
The old, made wise through suffering, pondered long,
   And paused, and feared to be deceived again—
Whilst some, of wild excitement weary, chose
Inglorious ease at once, and long repose.

LV.

Each one in turn, by his own angel led,
   Came to where Clotho's mystic webs were spun,

Next Atropos made firm the fatal thread,
   And wound the links which cannot be undone,
Then every spirit, helpless and alone,
Passed by Necessity's eternal throne.

LVI.

Er followed in their track, and reached the brink
   Of Lethe's ancient river, dark and deep;
Restrained himself, he saw his comrades drink,
   Then sink forgetful into death-like sleep;
But soon a tempest rose, and wrapped in night
Each slumbering phantom vanished from his sight.

LVII.

Yes,—but beyond the lightning's eager glare,
   Millions of shooting stars were seen to glow,
Freighted with souls in trance, they cleft the air,
   To breathe new life on the broad earth below,
Whilst with their rush the heavens were yet astir,
Blind Darkness gathered on the heart of Er.

LVIII.

That Darkness melts away: where is he? Lo!
   Beneath wild skies, which seem to reel and throb,
Pamphylia's well-known mountains ebb and flow
   Like giant clouds in storm—then, with a sob,
Upstarting, on his funeral pile he stood,
Recalled his dreams, and knew that all was good.

LIX.

Thence, on the wingèd winds, borne far and near,
    The tale of that divine uprising spread,
And the whole people gathered round to hear
    The voice of one recovered from the dead—
In haste, with double zeal, a man so dear
To God, as priest and monarch, to revere.

LX.

And though at length, by gracious death set free,
    His unreturning step left earth once more,
The hope he planted, like a stately tree,
    Stretched out its fruitful boughs from shore to shore,
And his great Legend, never waxing old,
On through the listening years in music rolled.

THE VETERANS OF THE GRAND ARMY MEETING NAPOLEON'S ASHES FROM ST. HELENA.

(FROM THÉOPHILE GAUTIER.)

BORED, and thus forced out of my room,
    Along the Boulevard I passed,
Around me hung December's gloom,
    The wind was cold, the showers drove fast.

Then straight I saw (how strange the sight!)
    Escaped from their grim dwelling-place,
Trampling through mud in sorry plight,
    Ghosts at mid-day, ghosts face to face.

Night is the time when shades have power,
    Whilst German moonlight silvers all,
Within some old and tottering tower,
    To flit across the pillared hall.

'Tis night when fairies from the floods
    In dripping robes rise like a breath,
Then drag beneath their lily buds
    Some boy whom they have danced to death.

'Twas night, if Zedlitz singeth true,
    When (half-seen shade) the Emperor
Marshalled in line, for that review,
    The shades of Austerlitz once more.

But spectres in the public street,
    Scarce from the playhouse paces two,
Veiled nor by mist, nor winding-sheet,
    Who stand there wearied and wet through.

Well may we wonder as we gaze;
    Three grumbling phantoms hover dim,
In uniform of other days,
    One ex-guard, two hussars with him.

Not these the slain, who, though they die,
    Still hear through earth Napoleon's drum;
But veterans of a time gone by
    Waked up to see his relics come.

Who, since that last, that fatal fight,
    Have grown, or fat, or lean and grim;
Whose uniforms, unless too tight,
    Float wide around each wasted limb.

Oh noble rags, still like a star
    To you the Cross of Honour clings,
Sublimely ludicrous, ye are
    Grander than purple worn by kings!

A nerveless plume, as if with fear,
    Trembles above the bearskin frayed;
Moth-fretted the pelisse is, near
    Those holes by hostile bullets made;

The leathern overalls, too large,
    Round the shrunk thigh in wrinkles fall,
And rusty sabres, wearying charge,
    Drag on the ground, or beat the wall.

The next one is grotesque, with chest
    Stretching a coat too small by half;
But for the stripes that deck his breast,
    At the old war-wolf we might laugh.

My brothers, mock them not too much;
    Rather salute, with heads low bent,
These heroes of an Iliad, such
    As Homer never could invent.

Greet each bald head with reverence due,
    For on brows, bronzed by many a clime,
A lengthening scar oft reddens through
    The lines that have been dug by time.

Their skins, by a strange blackness, tell
    Of Egypt's heat, and blinding light;
Russia's snow-powder, as it fell,
    Has kept those thin locks ever white.

Their hands may tremble; yes, still keen
    The cold of Beresina bites;
They limp, for long the march between
    Cairo and Wilna's frozen heights.

They droop, bent double, since in war
    No sheets but flags for sleep had they;
The helpless sleeve may flutter, for
    A round shot tore the arm away.

Laugh not, though round them leaps and jeers
    The howling street-boy with delight;
They were the day of those proud years,—
    The evening we—perchance the night.

They recollect, if we forget,
    Lancers in red, ex-guard in blue,
And worship, at his column met,
    The only God they ever knew.

Proud of the pains endured so long,
    Grateful for miseries nobly borne—
They feel the heart of France beat strong
    Under that clothing soiled and worn

Our tears then check the smile that played,
    To see this strange pomp on its way—
The Empire's ghostly masquerade—
    Dim as a ball when dawns the day.

Through skies which yet her splendours fill,
    The Eagle of our armies old,
From depths of glory, burning still,
      Spreads over them her wings of gold.

THE SPANISH MOTHER.

SUPPOSED TO BE RELATED BY A VETERAN FRENCH OFFICER.

YES! I have served that noble chief throughout his proud career,
And heard the bullets whistle past in lands both far and near—
Amidst Italian flowers, below the dark pines of the north,
Where'er the Emperor willed to pour his clouds of battle forth.

'Twas *then* a splendid sight to see, though terrible I ween,
How his vast spirit filled and moved the wheels of the machine,
Wide-sounding leagues of sentient steel, and fires that lived to kill,
Were but the echo of his voice, the body of his will.

But *now* my heart is darkened with shadows that rise and fall,
Between the sunlight and the ground to sadden and appal;

The woful things both seen and done, we heeded little then,
But they return, like ghosts, to shake the sleep of agèd men.

The German and the Englishman were each an open foe,
And open hatred hurled us back from Russia's blinding snow;
Intenser far, in blood-red light, like fires unquenched, remain
The dreadful deeds wrung forth by war from the brooding soul of Spain.

I saw a village in the hills, as silent as a dream,
Nought stirring but the summer sound of a merry mountain stream;
The evening star just smiled from heaven, with its quiet silver eye,
And the chestnut woods were still and calm, beneath the deepening sky.

But in that place, self-sacrificed, nor man nor beast we found,
Nor fig-tree on the sun-touched slope, nor corn upon the ground;—
Each roofless hut was black with smoke, wrenched up each trailing vine,
Each path was foul with mangled meat, and floods of wasted wine:

THE SPANISH MOTHER.

We had been marching, travel-worn, a long and burning way,
And when such welcoming we met after that toilsome day,
The pulses in our maddened breasts were human hearts no more,
But, like the spirit of a wolf, hot on the scent of gore.

We lighted on one dying man, they slew him where he lay,
His wife, close clinging, from the corpse they tore and wrenched away;
They thundered in her widowed ears, with frowns and cursings grim,
"Food, woman, food and wine, or else we tear thee limb from limb."

The woman shaking off *his* blood, rose raven-haired and tall,
And our stern glances quailed before one sterner far than all;
"Both food and wine," she said, "I have; I meant them for the dead,
"But ye are living still, and so let them be yours instead."

The food was brought, the wine was brought, out of a secret place,
But each one paused aghast, and looked into his neighbour's face;

Her haughty step and settled brow, and chill indifferent mien,
Suited so strangely with the gloom and grimness of the scene:

She glided here, she glided there, before our wondering eyes,
Nor anger showed, nor shame, nor fear, nor sorrow, nor surprise;
At every step from soul to soul a nameless horror ran,
And made us pale and silent as that silent murdered man.

She sate, and calmly soothed her child into a slumber sweet;
Calmly the bright blood on the floor crawled red around our feet;
On placid fruits and bread lay soft the shadows of the wine,
And we like marble statues glared—a chill unmoving line,

All white, all cold; and moments thus flew by without a breath,
A company of living things where all was still—but death—
My hair rose up from roots of ice, as there unnerved I stood
And watched the only thing that stirred—the ripple of the blood.

That woman's voice was heard at length, it broke the solemn spell,
And human fear displacing awe upon our spirits fell—

"Ho! slayers of the sinewless, ho! tramplers of the weak!
"What! shrink ye from the ghastly meats and life-bought
     wine ye seek?—

"Feed and begone, I wish to weep—I bring you out my
     store,
"Devour it—waste it all—and then, pass, and be seen no
     more—
"Poison! is that your craven fear?" she snatched a goblet up,
And raised it to her queen-like head, as if to drain the
     cup—

But our fierce leader grasped her wrist, "No! woman,
     no!" he said,
"A mother's heart of love is deep.—Give it your child
     instead."
She only smiled a bitter smile,—"Frenchman, I do not
     shrink,
"As pledge of my fidelity—behold the infant drink."—

He fixed on hers his broad black eye, scanning the inmost
     soul,
But her chill fingers trembled not as she returned the bowl.
And we, with lightsome hardihood dismissing idle care,
Sat down to eat and drink and laugh, over our dainty fare.

The laugh was loud around the board, the jesting wild and
     light—
But *I* was fevered with the march, and drank no wine that
     night;

I just had filled a single cup, when through my very brain
Stung, sharper than a serpent's tooth, an infant's cry of pain—

Through all that heat of revelry, through all that boisterous cheer,
To every heart its feeble moan pierced, like a frozen spear:
" Ay," shrieked the woman, darting up, " I pray you trust again
" A widow's hospitality, in our unyielding Spain.

" Helpless and hopeless, by the light of God Himself I swore
" To treat you as you treated *him*—that body on the floor.
" Yon secret place *I* filled, to feel, that if ye did not spare,
" The treasure of a dread revenge was ready hidden there.

" A mother's love is deep, no doubt, ye did not phrase it ill,
" But in your hunger, ye forgot that hate is deeper still.
" 'The Spanish woman speaks for Spain, for her butchered love the wife—
" To tell you, that an hour is all *my* vintage leaves of life."

I cannot paint the many forms by wild despair put on,
Nor count the crowded brave who sleep under a single stone;
I can but tell you, how before that horrid hour went by,
I saw the murderess beneath the self-avengers die—

But though upon her wrenchèd limbs they leapt like beasts of prey,
And with fierce hands as madmen tore the quivering life away,
Triumphant hate, and joyous scorn, without a trace of pain,
Burned to the last, like sullen stars, in that haughty eye of Spain.

And often now it breaks my rest, the tumult vague and wild,
Drifting, like storm-tost clouds, around the mother and her child—
While she, distinct in raiment white, stands silently the while,
And sheds through torn and bleeding hair the same unchanging smile.

GYTHIA.

A TALE OF THE LOWER EMPIRE.

I.

The cycle of the vultures, whom of old
   Great Romulus had numbered, one by one,
Whilst priest and prophet, on the heights, foretold
   How Rome's according centuries should run,
Drew slowly to its close—a time of woe,
   Plague, treason, bloodshed, famine, and despair:
Fierce earthquakes rent the tortured earth below;
   Above, the ancient heavens were deaf to prayer.
Their Gods were dead, and through that frozen gloom
Low voices muttered of man's coming doom.

II.

Over the empire, yet a mighty name,
   Armed anarchy hung ever, like a cloud,
Until that mockery of a throne became
   A living grave, the purple robe a shroud.
As on old ocean's waters, after storm,
   By blind and eager forces upward prest,

Each billow dies, when once its haughty form
    Hath towered in king-like pride above the rest;
So Cæsars rose—so fell to rise no more,
And broke like waves on Fate's unheeding shore.

III.

The golden land of Italy, once filled
    With her own sons, those warlike yeomen lords,
Who, in the bright Saturnian ages, tilled
    Their native soil, girt with their native swords,
Was now a prison-house, where men in chains,
    Scourged forth each morning from their cells, half-fed.
Went tottering over pestilential plains,
    That milk-white steeds or oxen might be bred
For some self-styled Patrician, whose dark skin
Hid not a drop of the old blood within.

IV.

The talons of Rome's eagle drooped unstrung,
    And weak the impulse of her withered wing;
Whilst nations closed around, whose hearts were young,
    And fresh with life as the first pulse of spring.
Yet, though her power waned fast, by gold and skill
    She bribed, or gulled, each chief who rose too high;
Tamed down barbaric tribes to work her will,
    And charmed the thunders of that angry sky
To vassal clouds, which formed a gorgeous pall
Around the dying sunset of her fall.

V.

Upon the edge of the wide Scythian plains,
   Stood Cherson, ever faithful, ever true;
Cæsar[1] himself she saved from death or chains,
   And at his call her savage kinsmen slew.
Therefore, among those wild Sauromatæ,
   A lodged and living principle of hate
Worked inwards, ever growing like a tree:
   They deemed that Cherson had arrested fate:
That, but for her, gems torn from shrieking Rome
Had lit the gloom of each Cimmerian home.

VI.

Revenge at first in open war they sought,
   Such war as neither babe nor mother spares;
But though, like fiends let loose from hell, they fought,
   Cherson's keen sword was sharper yet than theirs.
Hence foiled, and sore from failure, they began
   To hanker after triumph won by guile;
In the dark spirit shaping out a plan
   To stab through love, and murder with a smile.
Hence gentle words, hence gifts of price they bring,
And proffered marriage from their sullen king.

VII.

Cherson's old ruler, valiant Lamachus,
   Had seen his children perish, one by one:

---

[1] Constans.

A girl was left, his people's hope, so thus
    The Scythian message ran: "Behold my son.
"Give him the maiden Gythia. If thou wilt,
    "He shall become thy very own, and quit
"His father's house for ever: we have spilt
    "Enough of kindred blood; now let us knit
"Our tribes together in these bands of joy,
"Grant but thy daughter, I will send the boy.

VIII.

"Nay, more—lest in your hearts distrust should wake,
    "This do I offer, thus will I decree—
"Another chief his birthright here shall take,
    "And sway my Scythian clansmen after me;
"But steeds, and arms, and gold, and fragrant wine,
    "And silken robes, the half of all my store,
"He shall bear off across your frontier line,
    "Whilst we turn back, to see his face no more;
"Jars too divine, by friendly spirits made
"In the wise East, and talismans of jade.

IX.

"Thus ruled by brethren, let the nations live;
    "Forget this bitter bloodshed; quench their pride;
"Learn the new faith which teaches to forgive,
    "And in sweet peace, like bleating lambs, abide.
"Yea, let this peace grow strong, year after year,
    "By gifts and embassies between us sent,

"Till the lithe spider veils each shining spear,
  "And our dulled war-shafts crumble in the tent:
"So, through all time, that pair shall reverenced be,
"Like those twin stars which soothe the weary sea."

X.

Worn by long strife, and sated with renown,
  Like some old forest-tree about to fall,
Among his shadows, underneath the crown,
  Gray Lamachus mused ever in his hall:
Hushed voices seemed to thrill him as of old,
  The loved and lost in dreams went eddying past,
So that he yearned to hear and to behold
  Youth round him, ere he heard and looked his last:
His one keen hope to hear fair Gythia claim,
Before he died, a mother's happy name.

XI.

Hence, full of pleasant thoughts, consent he gave;
  For, in the storm of battle, oft the boy
Had flashed across him beautiful and brave:
  He welcomed him with all a warrior's joy;
And soon he said, "The children of my child
  "Again shall fill these halls with mirthful din."
The bridegroom answered merrily, and smiled—
  Smiled with his lips, to hide the heart within.
Till, like ripe fruit, from life the old man fell,
Was gathered to God's silence, and slept well.

XII.

Then spake the Lady Gythia, mastering grief:
"Because my father ever loved you all,
"Because ye also love your noble chief,
"Were it not good that a great festival
"Should keep his memory green and fresh for ever?
"By me let wine, and mead, and flesh be brought,
"And gold to fee sage bards, who may endeavour
"To sow among us seeds of noble thought;
"For I, the heir, am rich enough, ye know."
Then all the people answered, "Be it so."

XIII.

Thus in its season, for that solemn feast,
  She set before her tribe the best she had;
Rich sacrifice was offered by the priest,
  The wine-cup circled, and the land was glad.
Contending champions wrestled, ran, and rode;
  Contending bards poured hymns of triumph forth,
Whilst dance on dance, like headlong rivers, flowed,
  Lashed by the stormy music of the North:
All caution vanished, care aside was flung,
And the old revelled reckless as the young.

XIV.

Gythia's bold husband mingled with the crowd,
  Studied each humour, joined in every sport,

Then sent at night, unmarked and unavowed,
   A messenger to reach his father's court.
From that day forward ceaseless embassies
   To Cherson from their ancient foes were sent,
With gifts, with letters: thick as summer flies
   The stately Scythian warriors came and went—
Went, as it seemed, for in the blaze of day
They re-embarked, and steered their ships away.

XV.

Still there were those who muttered, "It is strange!
   "How often, when the winter moon is low,
"Light footfalls o'er the silent city range,
   "And sandalled steps indent the midnight snow!
"Up from our harbour to the palace gate
   "That sound glides past; the marks on that converge.
"We cannot tell why men should walk so late,
   "And fear that Gythia's serfs will need the scourge."
So talked they, but no stedfast watch was kept:
Serfs all seemed guiltless, and the mystery slept.

XVI.

Meanwhile the rolling months brought round again
   That feast; in blooms half-hid each temple smiled;
Sheep bleated, oxen lowed, wain after wain
   Groaned in with ivied casks at random piled.
It chanced a royal handmaid, for some fault,
   Spent those glad hours in prison all alone;

Beneath her dungeon stretched an ample vault,
　　Unused, unvisited, and hardly known :
For vast the palace was, with many a room
Left to itself in solitude and gloom.

XVII.

The bee-like murmur of the busy street
　　Soared up, and floated to those lonely towers ;
Fresh laughs throbbed round her, as on tiny feet
　　Children reeled by beneath a weight of flowers.
She turned her wheel, scarce knowing what she did,
　　And spun, but sung not as she sang of old,
Till from her careless fingers idly slid
　　The spindle—right across the floor it rolled
Like a thing guided, till it seemed to leap,
As if alive, into a crevice deep.

XVIII.

Her slack, indifferent hand was vaguely thrown
　　To reach it back, but it lay wedged so tight
She rose perforce to lift the fettering stone.
　　Why starts she back, with sudden horror white?
The halls below lay open to her ken :
　　There, like a swarm of hornets, just ere dawn,
Packed close and buzzing venom, mail-clad men
　　Muttered and frowned with swords already drawn,
The guests and envoys of the bygone year,
Armed and concealed—what bodes their presence here?

XIX.

She hung there numb with wonder, till at length
   Her heart gave one great bound, and with a jar,
The impulse of the truth, in all its strength,
   Flashed through her rapid as a shooting star:
She felt that these were they whose feet had crept
   Up from the shore along the midnight snow;
That the long peace had nought availed, except
   To change an open to a secret foe;
And the whole picture of their deadly scheme
Stood out before her, like a waking dream.

XX.

Soon as her evening meal was brought, the maid
   Seized on the bringer's hand, and held it fast:
With an intense and burning zeal, she prayed
   To see the Queen. When Gythia came at last,
Eager she spoke: "With thy unhappy slave
   "Deal, lady, as thou wilt—behold I kneel
"Before thee, reckless of myself, but save,
   "Oh save thy people from the Scythian steel!
"Treason lurks near thee; man that woman's heart,
"And though the flesh may shrink, perform thy part!"

XXI.

She spoke, and raised the stone. "Look, Gythia, look!"
   She cried, and showed those human hornets there;

The Queen's face rippled like a storm-swept brook,
  But her will froze it into calm despair.
The girl raved on: "A fire beyond control
  "Glows on my lips, through words that are not mine:
"Some god—some god has seized upon my soul:
  "His voice leaps through me, keen with life divine:
"His visions burn around, and, full of pain,
"Hurl their hot shadows on this eddying brain.

XXII.

"I see the Scythians come; 'Spare none!' they cry,
  "And the maimed corpses of unthinking men,
"Struck suddenly, beneath their onset lie.
  "Like lions hungry from a flooded fen,
"They bound together on the hapless town,
  "Whilst one, O Gythia! whom I dare not name,
"Shouts in fierce glee, 'Strike, strike the wretches down!
  "'Shed blood like water, scorch it dry with flame!'
"This is their future; but the heavenly powers,
"Who speak through me, have made the present ours.

XXIII.

"Death, death to us is what thy marriage meant!
  "Death at the feast, when the red wine is poured,
"Whilst all our hearts are light, our bows unbent,
  "The gate unguarded, hung away the sword!—
"This is the peace vouchsafed by Scythia's sons;
  "The love they proffer! Though a Scythian's bride,

"In those blue veins the blood of Cherson runs;
  "The form thy father gave thee cannot hide
"A false or feeble spirit; from his grave
"A murmur trembles forth—be true and brave!"

XXIV.

Stately and calm the Queen replied, "Away;
  "Thy faults are cancelled, and thy task is done;
"In our loved Cherson's cause, I too can say
  "If public needs wring forth the word, Spare none!"
So speaking, her proud feet glide through the halls,
  Watched at each step, and guided by her eyes,
She gains her royal chamber thus, and calls
  At once a council of the old and wise.
Then rising firm and undismayed, though pale,
She bows to each, and thus begins her tale:

XXV.

"Friends of my father, pillars of the state,
  "What bright hopes shone around my nuptial bed,
"Or seemed to shine, I need not here relate;
  "Enough to know that hope and truth are dead:
"The men we deal with nothing can restrain:
  "Gods are invoked, oaths plighted, temples built,
"Yea, children born of common blood, in vain.
  "But that revealing heaven lays bare their guilt,
"Our Scythian friends would now the dream fulfil
"Which for long years has kept their hatred still.

XXVI.

" Peace, gifts, and vows, e'en love itself they brought,
    " But all were false as hell; our ancient foes,
" From the first hour of compact, only sought
    " To trick us to destruction through repose :
" They have flocked here without a whisper, soft
    " As snow that droppeth, flake on flake, until
" The dumb mass, heaving in its cloud aloft,
    " Hangs ripe for ruin o'er the silent hill.
" Their hidden army thus waits but one breath,
" One utterance, to begin its work of death.

XXVII.

" We must anticipate that breath, outstrip
    " That utterance, and be first in action, ere
" The Prince, my loving husband, can let slip
    " Those dogs of hell to hunt us down like deer.
" In thought he triumphs well; but oft, we know,
    " The mocking destinies who sport with man,
" At some great purpose labouring firm and slow,
    " Veer round, and crush their half-completed plan :
" So, by the sea, blithe children toil in vain,
" To shape the sands, then dash them down again.

XXVIII.

" The Gods delight to startle and surprise ;
    " To show how light the proud, how weak the great ;

F

"How, at their nod, Hope shrivels up and dies,
   "Beneath the blighting irony of fate.
"Hence now, what we call chance, an idle name,
   "To the right spot, at the right moment, brings
"A simple girl, whose instincts put to shame
   "And foil the subtle stratagem of kings.
"That girl is here, to question if ye will!
"But the time presses—we may perish still."

XXIX.

The maid then summoned came without delay,
   Quick in her woman's wit, she made it clear,
How those false traitors seemed to sail away,
   But lurked in darkness, and in silence near;
How they returned, and straight were hidden down
   In those forgotten chambers, one and all,
Far from the keen eyes of the prying town,
   And the Queen's household, till the hour should call.
The council into wild confusion broke,
Loud clamouring, but once more their lady spoke.

XXX.

"Let no tumultuous passion of alarm
   "Thrill thro' the streets, and reach that hateful den.
"Like shadows flickering round, select and arm,
   "With stealthy swiftness, all our bravest men.
"They must creep past, along the palace wall,
   "And watch without a word: meanwhile I go

"To keep the feasting noisy in the hall,
  "And overmatch the sleek arch-traitor so."—
She spoke, and trusty chiefs, with fatal skill,
Go silent forth to execute her will.

XXXI.

The people revelled reckless, and at night
  They held the solemn banquet, as of old.
Along the rose-roofed galleries, perfumed light
  Flashed on a wilderness of gems and gold;
From golden flagons fragrant wine was poured,
  And mirth was loud—none merrier than the Queen;
All smiles, she faced her husband at the board,
  As if no shadow chilled the space between,
And with free spirit, whilst men talked and laughed,
From Cherson's royal cup she lightly quaffed.

XXXII.

That proud cup was an heirloom, brought from far,
  Some emperor's gift to one of her bold sires;
A sculptured vase of precious purple spar,
  Shot redly through with opalescent fires.
As in that dazzling blaze she raised it high,
  Its thin translucent texture flashed and gleamed
Above the tables, to each careless eye
  With generous grape-juice sparkling, as it seemed;
Yet it was strange how she forgot to shed
Their just libations to the noble dead.

XXXIII.

The young chief sat more silent, and at first
   Drank seldom—so at least his brain had planned.
But what avails against a Scythian thirst
   A Scythian purpose?   Powerless to withstand
The bright temptation of the bubbling wine,
   He tossed his beakers off—but suddenly,
Perchance admonished by some secret sign
   From friends at hand, he pushed the goblet by,
Stood up and spake : "A long-neglected vow
" Drives me, against my will, to leave you now.

XXXIV.

" The grim Diana of these northern plains [1]
   " Longs for some fresher blood than that which fills,
" With sleepy tingling stream, the sluggish veins
   " Of household bulls and goats ; our ancient hills
" Are loud with wolves, whom I have sworn to slay.
   " Bound by that oath, I rise at dawn, to stir
" Their dreams with steel, and on yon altar lay
   " Choice victims, worthy of myself and her.
" Pardon me then, I pray, each honoured guest,
" For I have left but little time for rest."

XXXV.

With courteous motion he departed, but,
   As his step died upon the distant stair,

---

[1]   —— ubi Taurica dirâ
    Cæde pharetratæ pascitur ara Deæ.—*Ovid*.

His wife broke forth: "Let all the doors be shut.
"'Tis well.—Now seize yon freedman loitering there
"And question him apart, nor let him dread
"A chiding, if his lord o'ersleep the day:
"I pledge my soul to rouse him from his bed
"When our staunch hounds are cheered upon their
    prey,
"Let him lie calm till then, it well may be
"Sweet sleep no more shall visit him nor me."

XXXVI.

Her face trembled with pain, while tears unshed
  Swam soft, and darkened those large earnest eyes;
In her clenched hand that chalice, frowning red,
  Burned, as the planet Mars, through misty skies,
Burns, breathing death to man: the electric strain
  Of fingers lithe, with ever-tightening clasp,
Pressed in, like flame, against the glittering grain,
  Till that strong crystal shivered in her grasp;
And the freed water, mocking wine no more,
Dropped white, through crimson rifts, along the floor.

XXXVII.

"Break thus, my heart!" rang forth her bitter cry;
  "Break, when thine hour is come; but now, oh soul,
"Toil on—nor claim the privilege to die."
  She dashed the fragments of that shattered bowl
Hard on the ground; then to her maids: "Be swift!
  "My royal robes, my father's sword and crown;

"The ancestral sceptre, reverenced as the gift
    "Of our ancestral God, bear deftly down;
"But let each Scythian treasure, prized of late,
"Rest here unmoved, and share the Scythian's fate."

XXXVIII.

Out of the hall she passed: her maidens there,
    With eager speed, glide through the tasks ordained:
For the last time she climbed the well-known stair;
    For the last time her bridal chamber gained;
Paused at the threshold of the darkened room,
    Then straight, with noiseless step, up to the bed
Slipped like a silent ghost across the gloom,
    And bent o'er him who slept her stately head.
Freed now from watching eyes, upon that face
Kisses unfelt, and tears she rained apace.

XXXIX.

"Oh thou!" she cried, "who in these arms of mine
    "Hast lived, for whom alone this heart has beat,
"Farewell! farewell! Not e'en through help divine
    "Our spirits in a better land may meet!
"The river of thy youthful blood must roll
    "A gulf impassable between, and sever
"Our two eternities, body and soul:
    "In this last kiss I take my leave for ever:
"Doomed, e'en beyond the grave, in shades forlorn,
"By doubts which die not, to be racked and torn.

XL.

"Whether thy love were wholly false, or whether,
　"Had not thy father trained thee as our foe,
"Blighting both hearts, we might have been together
　"All that we seemed—I never now shall know.
"That bitter yearning, like a tainted gale,
　"Must mix itself through time with every breath;
"Yea, still unquenched, when time itself shall fail,.
　"Sting life immortal into living death.
"Oh! for one word, through slumbering lips apart,
"To shrine for ever in the solaced heart."

XLI.

She listened, with a sudden wish to spare,
　But the word came not: if he spake of aught,
If that low muttering can a meaning bear,
　Still seems it with his hoped-for treason fraught.
Her mouth was stern at once, her tears were dried,
　Her shaken purpose reassumed its sway;
Her eyes grew fierce, and rising in her pride,
　Without another word she passed away.
The stars on him poured down an evil gleam
When that last whisper issued from his dream.

XLII.

Then said she to her friends, who gathered round,
　"This is no midnight murder which we plan,

"But a great act of justice: robed and crowned,
 "I shall give sentence before God and man.
"I call my father's spirit to my heart;
 "I clothe myself for judgment, like a queen;
"Fix then our canopy from all apart
 "Before yon shrine, that I may stand serene
"Beneath the conscious heavens, and call on them
"To wing my words with life as I condemn."

XLIII.

Thence, when her orders were fulfilled, alone
 She passed, in gloom and silence, like a cloud,
To take her place on Cherson's ancient throne.
 There ran a tremor through the listening crowd
As that pale woman bound her brows about
 With the gemmed circle worn by kings of old,
And, as the sign of rightful power, stretched out
 Her mystic staff of sky-descended gold:[1]
"Hear, Heaven," she cried; "give ear, thou Stygian gloom,
"And ratify what I pronounce for doom.

XLIV.

"If Truth and Law, unending, uncreate,
 "Ere light was born, the realms of ether trod;[2]
"If their pure essence, fused through time and fate,
 "Sustain the everlasting youth of God—
"Then let your vengeance fall on those, ye Powers,
 "Who trample them to dust with atheist scorn;

---

[1] *Vide* Herodotus, Book iv.
[2] *Vide* Sophocles, Œd. Tyrannus.

"Let their souls, wandering on thro' anguished hours,
    "Lament for ever that they once were born,
"And learn too late, in Death's abysmal deep,
    "That God's high justice only seems to sleep."

XLV.

So, from her place on high, the judgment fell
    Intense with earnest prayer and awful rites,
Whilst jet-black steers bled to the lords of hell:
    Next, at her bidding, fifty chosen knights,
Equipped with torches fiercely burning, roam
    About the palace, and those fires apply,
Till the huge timbers of that wild old home
    In fifty places flare against the sky;
And the whole people, 'wildered at the sight,
Stood mute and livid in that broadening light.

XLVI.

High rose the roaring flames, and far away,
    As the wild Northern meteor shakes and shines,
Their blood-red shadows wavered o'er the bay
    And scared the owl beneath her covering pines.
Meanwhile, all motionless in shining steel,
    The mute avengers watch each secret door:
As forth, half dead, the hidden traitors reel,
    Their swords upraised flash once, and all is o'er.
Gone that foul plot, like mist before the sun;
Of those grim traitors there remains but one.

XLVII.

He unaware slept still, but the hot smoke
    And the sharp crackling sounds which throbbed and rung,
Like jets of hail, upon his slumber broke:
    In dreamy wonder from his couch he sprung,
And sought the stair—between that stair and him
    There raged a burning sea! In fierce despair
He dashes back through smoke-wreaths whirling dim,
    At the broad window—what beholds he there?
A nation massed for battle, calm and still,
And the wild fires allowed to work their will.

XLVIII.

Yea, more—before the Temple's haughty gate,
    The sceptre of the law within her hand,
Sat Gythia, like the statue of a Fate,
    As priestess, judge, and monarch of the land.
His eyeballs, rolling round in wild amaze,
    A glance half hate and half inquiry throw;
Whilst, keen and clear, framed in that crimson blaze,
    Pale Gythia's answering eyeballs glared below:
Then, folding both his arms in silent pride,
Like a trapped wolf, the dauntless traitor died.

XLIX.

So perished that fell purpose, nursed and fed
    Through years of patient craft. First from his cell

The trembling freedman of the Prince was led;
  They spared him only, the grim tale to tell.
By this, the vengeful fires had ceased to burn;
  So the wife took her husband's bones, and laid
Them, silken-folded, in a golden urn:
  "Let Scythia take her offspring back," she said;
"False to his vows—to God—to this fond breast,
"He yet was true to her—there let him rest."

L.

Time soon rolled on through Cherson as of yore:
  They swept the palace ashes far away,
Rearing high domes even statelier than before;
  But the Queen's heart in its hot embers lay,
With none to build it up. The voice of fame
  Dropped on the gap that crumbled there, like rain,
To sting, not quench, that slow but wasting flame;
  Till murmurs rose, Why cherish this dull pain?
Can Cherson saved no touch of rapture bring?
Is praise immortal so contemned a thing?

LI.

Then spake the Lady Gythia, mastering grief:
  "My people's truth I know; will they do all
"I ask, to give this aching brain relief?
  "At once, from woman's hopes and dreams I fall,
"Like that scorched rock which Jupiter of old,
  "On our scared fields, a fiery portent, hurled,

"Which now, all lost and lonely, we behold,
  "A lifeless alien in man's living world—
"So am I flung from heaven—my heaven—to live,
"If life it be, when earth has nought to give.

LII.

"Still some deep draught of glory may be mine;
  "Compared with love, that wine is cold and thin;
"Yet on the eye its burning bubbles shine,
  "And their keen flash may pierce the clouds within.
"By chiefs and people let an oath be sworn,
  "An oath to highest Jove, that, when I die,
"This body shall with noble rites be borne,
  "'Neath your mid-market's hurrying feet to lie,
"Whilst, on a column, with fit words engraved,
"My image guards the city that I saved.

LIII.

"So, through the few pale years which yet remain,
  "On its proud future shall the soul be fed,
"And feel, at every pang, that not in vain
  "The nerves have quivered, and the heart has bled.
"Childless and husbandless from earth I go,
  "To freeze alone in Death's unpitying clime;
"My deeds my children are, and they must show
  "That Gythia was not barren in her time:
"Of infant laughs, of peace, of hope bereft,
"Though fame be nothing, fame alone is left."

LIV.

Then, whilst her chieftains, as she bade them, swore,
   Whilst crowds applauding ratified the boon,
Faint lights of joy touched at her heart once more,
   Like the chill rainbows of a waning moon;
The common paths of life once more she trod,
   Changed wool for vintage of Ionian isles,
Led up her firstlings to the common God,
   And smiled, with somewhat cold and weary smiles,
Till, in their dusty present, most grew blind
To the past tempest drifting off behind.

LV.

Gythia's uprooted heart, her blasted powers,
   And the huge impact of that awful deed,
Sank low, within each slight growth of the hours,
   As a felled oak-tree amid fern and weed:
There came a doubt upon her spirit then;
   Like a low mist, around her coiled and crept
Distrust of self, distrust of fellow-men;
   The motive faded, the pang never slept.
"When memory dies, when hope and fear are gone,
"Why," thought she, " should their gratitude live on?"

LVI.

"I have heard, somewhere, the wild legend told
   "Of a fierce hunter, who, in hunger sore,

"His birthright for a mess of pottage sold;
　"I, at as low a rate, have sold yet more,
"And now I will be paid—they shall not walk,
　"In their fine scorn, above my nameless grave,
"Sneer at my sex, and of the beldame talk
　"Who claimed things never claimed by warrior brave;
"As if dull sworders, only fit to strike,
"And woman, under impulse, were alike."

LVII.

Thenceforth she shut herself from all apart;
　Her servants sorrowed in the streets, and said
How leech-craft could not reach a broken heart,
　And that their lady was as good as dead.
The people would have grieved, but that a blight
　Sat on each field, and scorched all fruits like fire:
The nobles might have mourned her, but the sight
　Of a realm vacant, kindled fierce desire.
The poor, absorbed in losses of their own,
Forgot: the great were wrestling for a throne.

LVIII.

Hence, when the message came that she was gone,
　It seemed no more the public heart to shake
Than a mute rain-drop, when it falls upon
　Vexed waters, will disturb a mountain lake.
Her vassals brought a marble likeness forth:
　"Where," asked they, "is this image to be placed?

"She hoped in death still to defy the North,
  "And frown for ever at yon Scythian waste."
The chiefs replied, "She heedeth nothing now;
"It were not good to keep so wild a vow,

LIX.

"Lest those to come should sneer at us, and say,
  "'These men of Cherson were but feeble folk,
"'A woman was their hero—she bore sway;
  "'They crouched, like slave-girls, underneath her yoke.'
"Although we loved her well, this may not be;
  "Enough, forsooth, that at this funeral
"Bards shall sing praises; that, by our decree,
  "The senate will be present, one and all,
"Whilst she is laid her father's tomb within,
"To sleep, like others, near her kith and kin."

LX.

So her friends bore their baffled statue home,
  Defrauded of its column in the street;
And built a pyre, beneath her central dome,
  Of mighty trees, rich gums, and incense sweet;
But, though her damsels shrieked and tore their hair,
  And sobbed, few tears in truth were seen to flow;
Looks, full of meaning, lived among them there,
  And stealthy smiles passed flitting to and fro;
The elders chided, but, to ears that heard,
Something rang hollow in each angry word;

LXI.

On the third morn the gates were opened wide;
    In a huge car the pyre was fixed; on high
Lay Gythia's form, clothed richly, like a bride,
    With its veiled face turned upwards to the sky:
So through the streets they passed, a gorgeous throng,
    For priests, and senators, and soldiers came,
And bards, who chanted forth a solemn song
    To an old burthen, honouring Gythia's name;
Till, at her father's tomb, within the porch,
That car stood still—the high priest raised his torch.

LXII.

Lo! at his feet the corpse's veil is flung,
    And Gythia, bright with anger and with scorn,
Like flame from a volcano, upward sprung:
    "For this then all my bitter life was borne!
"For this my soul I stabbed!" she cried. "No longer
    "To faith, or truth, or gratitude I trust—
"These have no place on earth; but God is stronger
    "Than you, I trow, poor clods of dreaming dust;
"I spring from God: this sceptre of my sires,
"Which I grasp still, congealed from heavenly fires.[1]

LXIII.

"They sleep within it still—beware! I know
    "The skies will hear their daughter, if she call."

[1] For the legend of the burning gold that fell from heaven, *see* Herod. book iv.

As her words burst like thunder, thunders low
    Echoed them in the dark aërial hall:
The crowd dropped prostrate, as if from above
    A sudden sunstroke through her eyes had leapt.
"Even yet I live to learn," she said: "is love
    "So light when weighed with terror?" and she wept.
But the crowd slunk in shamefaced silence off,
And the hard nobles were too wise to scoff.

LXIV.

Once more the common paths of life she trod,
    Changed wool for vintage of Ionian isles,
Led up her firstlings to their common God,
    And smiled, with somewhat cold and weary smiles:
But now her people, with unsleeping dread,
    Revered their more than human Queen—they knew
The shadow of her curse hung overhead;
    As the couched partridge, trembling through and through,
Feels, though she see not, poised in gloomy rest,
The kite's huge wings above her twittering nest.

LXV.

So thus, from year to year, subdued of soul,
    And bent to do her bidding, they remained;
Till, when the grave reclaimed her, to that goal
    She went, well knowing that her end was gained.
Then rose that column in their market-place;
    Fit words were graven on its polished stones;

Whilst Gythia's form, alive with angry grace,
   Towered high above her consecrated bones.
Such Gythia's tale—so, when her course was run,
That earthly immortality she won.

LXVI.

But Time is strong on this wild globe of ours,
   And immortalities, which seem designed
To bloom for ever, fade like summer flowers;
   Beneath the autumn rain and winter wind,
That column, with its statue, sunk to dust;
   The people that upreared them ceased to be:
Nations, and tribes, and languages were thrust
   Each over each, as by some sweeping sea;
Till battles of our own rocked to and fro,
O'er the forgotten brave, who sleep below.

LXVII.

Moreover, that fresh glory, though we think
   That, like the unwearied sun, its light shall last,
At God's good pleasure must unheeded sink
   Into a moonless and a starless past;
For an hour cometh when the gulf between
   Gythia and Inkerman seems but a day;
All will have changed upon this busy scene,
   And Britain's self, like Gythia, passed away—
So that for us, and her, rare students look
In some dull chronicler's unfingered book.

HOW LORD NAIRN WAS SAVED.

Of the six condemned peers, Lord Nairn is said to have been saved by the personal interposition of Stanhope. They had been at Eton together, and Stanhope bore down all opposition to his request, by threatening to resign. See Lord Mahon's *History*, vol. i.

The story is supposed to be told by a Jacobite Etonian of the day.

  As, under eddying Baltic flaws,
    Which chase the soft southwest away,
  Through each rash blossom, flame-like, gnaws
    The icy blight of May—
  So Fortune, with a bitter breath,
    (Just as her beauty budded forth),
  Swept, cankered into dusty death,
    Our white rose of the north.
Whilst names, which seemed oak-rooted in their place,
Like homeless winds, went fleeting into space.

  Caerlaverock's halls in silence stand,
    And "Kenmure's lads are men" in vain;
  The best blood of Northumberland
    Makes rich the London rain.
  In ghastly sympathy with him
    Whose feet shall cross its bridge no more,

HOW LORD NAIRN WAS SAVED.

Dilstone's weird moat, an omen grim,
 Flows, dark with phantom gore.[1]
Long shall each Cumbrian boor recall the sign,
Which boded ruin to that ancient line.

 A prince, who speaks no English, spares
  None that have loyal blood to shed;
 Still, not through that cabal of theirs,
  Is English impulse dead.
 When to his block the Elector vowed
  Bold Nairn's unshrinking head to give,
 Stanhope, in generous anger loud,
  Swore that his friend should live;
That neither title, pension, place, nor star,
Should buy, from him, that head for Temple Bar.

 Sleek Walpole strove in vain to bring
  His bribes to bear; in vain the lout,
 Whom Whigs now call an English king,
  Threw German oaths about.
 Back from the fields of boyhood came
  The past, with all its hopes, once more;
 The passion of each hard-fought game,
  The rustling of the oar,
As, where the yellow river-lilies float,
Round the tall rushes whirled their eager boat.

---

[1] The moat at Dilstone Castle, the chief seat of the Derwentwater Radcliffes, is reported to have suddenly assumed the appearance of blood on the morning of Lord Derwentwater's execution.

Once more he sees two lads, at eve,
　　Who dream of glory, side by side;
Each strange web that their fancies weave,
　　Too loving then to hide.
Under the whispering elms they walk,
　　With arms around each other twined,
And, rapt into the future, talk,
　　To future sorrow blind :
Then pale that well-known face seemed hovering nigh,
And blood drops fell, as some one raised it high.

"I brook on this point no control,"
　　He shouted; "seek not to reply;
"For by that God, who made the soul,
　　"I will not have him die.
"What, use me, ruthless as a tool,
　　"To slay my earliest friend? our names
"Are cut together in the school,
　　"Together at my dame's;
"Half of my past is his, half his is mine;
"I will not hear it argued.　I resign."

When that word thundered through the throng
　　Of supple slaves, they could not choose;
A soldier-statesman he, too strong
　　For clerks like them to lose.
So Walpole, with the heart of stone,
　　Before that righteous outbreak bent,

And George, like dog forced from his bone,
　　Growled forth a grim consent.
Our turn will come—we must not then forget,
One rebel, true to Eton memories yet.

MEHRAB KHAN.

"Mehrab Khan died, as he said he would, sword in hand, at the door of his own Zenana."—*Capture of Kelat.*

WITH all his fearless chiefs around,
    The Moslem leader stood forlorn,
And heard at intervals, the sound
    Of drums athwart the desert borne.
To him a sign of fate, they told
    That Britain in her wrath was nigh,
And his great heart its powers unrolled
    In steadiness of will to die.

"Ye come, in your mechanic force,
    "A soulless mass of strength and skill—
"Ye come, resistless in your course,
    "What matters it?—'Tis but to kill.
"A serpent in the bath, a gust
    "Of venomed breezes through the door,
"Have power to give us back to dust—
    "Has all your grasping empire more?

" Your thousand ships upon the sea,
   " Your guns and bristling squares by land,
" Are means of death—and so may be
   " A dagger in a damsel's hand.
" Put forth the might you boast, and try
   " If it can shake my seated will;
" By knowing when, and how to die,
   " I can escape, and scorn you still.

" The noble heart, as from a tower,
   " Looks down on life that wears a stain;
" He lives too long, who lives an hour
   " Beneath the clanking of a chain.
" I breathe my spirit on my sword,
   " I leave a name to honour known,
" And perish, to the last the lord
   " Of all that man can call his own."

Such was the mountain leader's speech;
   Say ye, who tell the bloody tale,
When havoc smote the howling breach,
   Then did the noble savage quail?
No—when through dust, and steel, and flame,
   Hot steams of blood, and smothering smoke,
True as an arrow to its aim,
   The meteor-flag of England broke;

And volley after volley threw
   A storm of ruin, crushing all,

Still cheering on a faithful few,
    He would not yield his father's hall.
At his yet unpolluted door
    He stood, a lion-hearted man,
And died, A FREEMAN STILL, before
    The merchant thieves of Frangistan.

THE RED THREAD OF HONOUR.

TOLD TO THE AUTHOR BY
THE LATE SIR CHARLES JAMES NAPIER.

ELEVEN men of England
  A breast-work charged in vain;
Eleven men of England
  Lie stripped, and gashed, and slain.
Slain; but of foes that guarded
  Their rock-built fortress well,
Some twenty had been mastered,
  When the last soldier fell.

Whilst Napier piloted his wondrous way
  Across the sand-waves of the desert sea,
Then flashed at once, on each fierce clan, dismay,
  Lord of their wild Truckee.[1]
These missed the glen to which their steps were bent,
  Mistook a mandate, from afar half heard,
And, in that glorious error, calmly went
  To death without a word.

[1] A stronghold in the Desert, supposed to be inaccessible and impregnable.

The robber-chief mused deeply,
  Above those daring dead;
"Bring here," at length he shouted,
  "Bring quick, the battle thread.
"Let Eblis blast for ever
  "Their souls, if Allah will:
"But WE must keep unbroken
  "The old rules of the Hill.

"Before the Ghiznee tiger
  "Leapt forth to burn and slay;
"Before the holy Prophet
  "Taught our grim tribes to pray;
"Before Secunder's lances
  "Pierced through each Indian glen;
"The mountain laws of honour
  "Were framed for fearless men.

"Still, when a chief dies bravely,
  "We bind with green *one* wrist—
"Green for the brave, for heroes,
  "ONE crimson thread we twist.
"Say ye, oh gallant Hillmen,
  "For these, whose life has fled,
"Which is the fitting colour,
  "The green one, or the red?"

"Our brethren, laid in honoured graves, may wear
  "Their green reward," each noble savage said;

"To these, whom hawks and hungry wolves shall tear,
 "Who dares deny the red?"

Thus conquering hate, and stedfast to the right,
 Fresh from the heart that haughty verdict came;
Beneath a waning moon, each spectral height
 Rolled back its loud acclaim.

Once more the chief gazed keenly
 Down on those daring dead;
From his good sword their heart's blood
 Crept to that crimson thread.
Once more he cried, "The judgment,
 "Good friends, is wise and true,
"But though the red *be* given,
 "Have we not more to do?

"These were not stirred by anger,
 "Nor yet by lust made bold;
"Renown they thought above them,
 "Nor did they look for gold.
"To them their leader's signal
 "Was as the voice of God:
"Unmoved, and uncomplaining,
 "The path it showed they trod.

"As, without sound or struggle,
 "The stars unhurrying march,
"Where Allah's finger guides them,
 "Through yonder purple arch,

THE RED THREAD OF HONOUR.

"These Franks, sublimely silent,
   "Without a quickened breath,
"Went, in the strength of duty,
   "Straight to their goal of death.

"If I were now to ask you,
   "To name our bravest man,
"Ye all at once would answer,
   "They called him Mehrab Khan.
"He sleeps among his fathers,
   "Dear to our native land,
'With the bright mark he bled for
   "Firm round his faithful hand.

"The songs they sing of Roostum
   "Fill all the past with light;
"If truth be in their music,
   "He was a noble knight.
"But were those heroes living,
   "And strong for battle still,
"Would Mehrab Khan or Roostum
   "Have climbed, like these, the Hill?"

And they replied, "Though Mehrab Khan was brave,
   "As chief, he chose himself what risks to run;
'Prince Roostum lied, his forfeit life to save,
   "Which these had never done."

   "Enough!" he shouted fiercely;
     "Doomed though they be to hell,

"Bind fast the crimson trophy
　"Round BOTH wrists—bind it well.
"Who knows but that great Allah
　"May grudge such matchless men,
"With none so decked in heaven,
　"To the fiends' flaming den?"

Then all those gallant robbers
　Shouted a stern "Amen!"
They raised the slaughter'd sergeant,
　They raised his mangled ten.
And when we found their bodies
　Left bleaching in the wind,
Around BOTH wrists in glory
　That crimson thread was twined.

Then Napier's knightly heart, touched to the core,
　Rung, like an echo, to that knightly deed,
He bade its memory live for evermore,
　That those who run may read.

THE PRIVATE OF THE BUFFS.

"Some Seiks, and a private of the Buffs, having remained behind with the grog-carts, fell into the hands of the Chinese. On the next morning they were brought before the authorities, and commanded to perform the *kotou*. The Seiks obeyed; but Moyse, the English soldier, declaring that he would not prostrate himself before any Chinaman alive, was immediately knocked upon the head, and his body thrown on a dunghill."—*See China Correspondent of the " Times."*

Last night, among his fellow roughs,
 He jested, quaffed, and swore;
A drunken private of the Buffs,
 Who never looked before.
To-day, beneath the foeman's frown,
 He stands in Elgin's place,
Ambassador from Britain's crown,
 And type of all her race.

Poor, reckless, rude, low-born, untaught,
 Bewildered, and alone,
A heart, with English instinct fraught,
 He yet can call his own.
Ay, tear his body limb from limb,
 Bring cord, or axe, or flame:
He only knows, that not through *him*
 Shall England come to shame.

THE PRIVATE OF THE BUFFS.

Far Kentish[1] hop-fields round him seem'd,
    Like dreams, to come and go;
Bright leagues of cherry-blossom gleam'd,
    One sheet of living snow;
The smoke, above his father's door,
    In gray soft eddyings hung:
Must he then watch it rise no more,
    Doom'd by himself, so young?

Yes, honour calls!—with strength like steel
    He put the vision by.
Let dusky Indians whine and kneel;
    An English lad must die.
And thus, with eyes that would not shrink,
    With knee to man unbent,
Unfaltering on its dreadful brink,
    To his red grave he went.

Vain, mightiest fleets of iron framed;
    Vain, those all-shattering guns;
Unless proud England keep, untamed,
    The strong heart of her sons.
So, let his name through Europe ring—
    A man of mean estate,
Who died, as firm as Sparta's king,
    Because his soul was great.

[1] The Buffs, or East Kent Regiment.

DEMOSTHENES.

Τίς οὕτως εὐήθης ἐστὶν ὑμῶν ὅστις ἀγνοεῖ τον ἐκεῖθεν πόλεμον δεῦρο ἥξοντα, ἂν ἀμελήσωμεν;—DEM., *Olynthiac I.*

SONNET I.

A GRIM Power in the north rose up and spread,
Slowly at first, then as a forest-fire
Gnaws its way on through reed and fern and briar,
Till round huge tree-trunks, like an ocean red,
It billows, and the stained sky overhead
Is filled with lights of ruin, marching nigher—
So the war-flame crept forward; yet fools said,
It has so far to come, it needs must tire
Long ere our homes are reached. Eat, drink, and play!
So those who ruled, as we rule now, the seas,
The men of Athens, prattled in their day;
Yet one true seer rebuked that reckless ease,
(Oh that the Death-king, from the Death-world gray,
For us would raise him up) Demosthenes!

SONNET II.

He, prophet-like, beheld the coming years
As from a tower, and to the crowd below
Spake ever of that keen unresting foe;

But, prophet-like, he spake to heedless ears;
"As if the men of Macedon were peers
"To us," they cried; "you ask us to forego
"Music and dance—the comedy that cheers,
"The tragic song that sheds a deathless glow
"Round old heroic names—only to check
"Some inroad on the barbarous wilds of Thrace.
"Such triumphs weaken—then let Philip wreck
"His fortunes, grappling there with endless space;
"He will not set his foot upon our neck;
"For loved Athene guards her dwelling-place."

SONNET III.

So that wild Thrace—the Turkestan of old—
Teaches Emathian peasants how to fight;
Not in philosophy take they delight,
But better than all Stoics, heat and cold
They bear unmoved—and die when they are told:
Till all their king had learnt—to the full height
Of Art, and Theban[1] discipline, they hold.
Soon a huge army towers in all men's sight,
A dull mass of barbarians, yet trained true
In the whole skill of Hellas—More than all,
Against the over-civilised and few,
From their rough hills they gather strong and tall,
Couch longer lances, bursting armies through;
And face the battle like a living wall.

[1] I need scarcely say that Philip, when young, was carefully instructed in the art of war by Epaminondas.

SONNET IV.

But yet that pass by the Thessalian sea,
Where the three hundred gave their lives away,
Stands fast, and bars the conqueror's destined way.
So long as Athens guards it jealously
Philip is checked, and trembling Hellas free:
But the great God of Delphi joins the fray,
Apollo tells mankind, "They come for me;
"I summon Philip,[1]—Philip must obey."
No love of native land—no thoughts of what
The hour at hand may bring, are lawful now;
As for the impious Phocians, spare them not,
They must be crushed—what can it matter how?
On Philip, as God's instrument, the lot
Has fallen—join with him to strike the blow.

SONNET V.

"True, Philip may have erred; but now at least
"Avenger of Apollo, and attired
"In the bright robes of zeal, like one inspired,
"He moves to war—a dedicated priest.
"We cannot aid the Phocians—they have ceased
"To rank with men—our ears and hearts are tired
"By selfish talks of Attic interest—
"The God—the God—on monsters that are hired

---

[1] Philip was appointed commander, by the intrigues of his partisans in Greece, against the Phocians in the so-called sacred war, and again against the Locrians of Amphissa, who were supposed to have also incurred the wrath of Apollo somewhat later.

"With his own wealth against his shrine to fight
"Vengeance must sweep—and those unspeakable
"Rebels who hate the Lord of life and light
"Must perish.   Philip's holy sword works well:
"With his most virtuous efforts now unite."
These pious words from our good Phocion fell.

SONNET VI.

And so at length, of help and hope bereft,
Phalæcus,[1] having wasted all his gold,
And caring little what it was he sold,
To the fierce Macedonians open left
Thermopylæ, the Dardanelles of old—
What recked he of the path by which he cleft
His way to safety?   Thus then, uncontrolled,
Philip, after long cat-like creepings deft,
Rose up erect *within the Pass*—and smiled.
Can Athens win from that hard hand release?
No.   'Twas too late.   Soon, with free blood defiled,
There fell on man what Phocion called a peace,
When Pindar's house looked round on ruins wild
At Thebes—and dim shames veiled the "eye of Greece."

SONNET VII.

Then, whilst the Son of Ammon from the west
Swept like a proud wave, which the earthquake pours

---

[1] Phalæcus, the last general of the Phocians, unable to defend Thermopylæ without ships, and being abandoned by Athens, delivered it up to Philip on certain terms.

From the vext sea high over wasted shores,
Hellas sank down, and moaned in gloomy rest—
Her place in history gone. Yet undeprest,
Demosthenes, a quenchless spirit, soars
Towards Freedom's star—still hoping for the best—
He trusts in Time—in Space—in private hate—
He trusts that Death may open wide her doors
To let the Titan conqueror through—and then,
As the huge sceptre drops (a load too great
To be upreared by hands of smaller men),
Greece may once more rise mistress of her fate,
And Honour's voice be heard on earth again.

SONNET VIII.

Alas! the dry-rot of the heart spreads wide,
If noble zealots yet for freedom yearn,
Lost opportunities can ne'er return:
Though the great savage crowned and deified,
At Babylon may sink to dust, or burn
Like common men, the harsh Fates have denied
To those in whom all loftier thoughts have died,
The power to call them back at will, and learn
To wear the mighty armour of the Past
On shaking limbs, with spirits shrunken low.
One poor defeat[1] has scattered them as fast
As clouds before the driving north wind go;
And the strong man sees certain death at last
Before him—half rejoicing it is so.

[1] Crannon—a trifling battle in itself, but sufficient to dissolve the Grecian confederacy against Antipater.

SONNET IX.

From Great Poseidon's altar looking back
Through the long years, his work to him seemed good.
There was no spot upon the solemn track
That lay behind; yea, though the air was black
With cloud and tempest not to be withstood,
His Past lay safe from thunder, and endued
With grander immortality than aught
That shines round conquering footsteps drenched in blood.
Once more he foiled in thought the fierce attack,
And to his lips the oath that sent a thrill
Through Time, and liveth yet in light, was brought.
True then, that God-like utterance is true still,
Ay, let Antipater the body kill,
He cannot reach the soul, or gain the end he sought.

SONNET X.

Yet this man,[1] the mean Roman satirist,
In most unroman temper, meanly blames,
Because, forsooth, a few short years were missed.
Ay, if all higher hopes had been dismissed,
If on enslaved Olynthus, wrapt in flames,
He had looked calm, with ruthless eye, and hissed
Each orator who urged his country's claims,
He might have witnessed new Olympian games
Ruled over by some man of Macedon.
He might have culled his olives, pressed his wine,

[1] Juvenal.

Seen savage spears around the Parthenon
(Good Phocion looking on) drawn up in line—
With Issus held for Salamis divine,
And Gaugamela mocking Marathon.

SONNET XI.

But he preferred to go: then Demades,
Fingering his Darics—Phocion good, misguided
By self-deceiving virtues—both derided
The man who gave up health and wealth and ease,
Yea life, for Athens. "This Demosthenes,"
Sneered the base rhetorician, "slow, one-sided,
"Although he drained his heart to win and please,
"Could never speak with power off-hand as I did."
So passed they careless on, as if the spark
Of that bright life had but gleamed forth and gone,
Devoured, like summer lightning, by the dark.
Yet other thoughts perchance were theirs anon,
When Demades, that rash, ill-fated clerk,
From his own letter[1] shrank—aghast and wan.

SONNET XII.

Perchance a death sought nobly, and sustained
By golden thoughts and sacred memories,
Seemed better than the one which caught him, stained
With treason to his race, and black engrained

---

[1] A letter from Demades was forwarded to Antipater, which he made him read, and then sent him to execution.

To the heart's core—More than Demosthenes
By all his rapid eloquence, his lies,
His unabashed self-seeking, has he gained?
No; vile in vain, by a worse fate he dies.
And what of Phocion? let us turn away,
Nor watch how public hatred, like a fire,
Roars round the man delivered as a prey
By those he leaned on—to the crowd's desire.
He tried to save his country, we will say,
"By Virtue," but what Vice wrought ends more dire?

LADY AGNES.

This story is quoted by Mr. Ferrier in his *Theory of Apparitiosn*, from Barton's *Anatomy of Melancholy*.

It is the hour, when through the air
   The Elves of silence creep,
And maidens, with unbraided hair,
   Sink into blooming sleep.

The Lady Agnes, lightly lifting
   Her dove-like hazel eyes,
From room to room, like sunlight shifting,
   To her calm chamber hies.

Beautiful Agnes! as she went
   By stair and gallery wall,
There seemed a mellowing glory lent
   Unto that wild old hall.

Even portraits, grim with iron thought,
   And monsters of the loom,
Were softened, as if near her, nought
   Could keep its natural gloom.

But as her youthful beauty stole
    Through the long corridor,
There spread a passion on her soul,
    Shadowing its brightness o'er.

Her eye, among the imaged dead
    No face of love could see—
"Alas for her who died," she said,
    "In giving life to me.

"These warrior portraits stern and old,
    "Make sad this echoing place;
"It would have soothed me to behold
    "My mother's angel face.

"But she was taken suddenly
    "From human hope and fear,
"And lives but in the memory
    "Of those who loved her here.

"But I, who never saw her—I
    "Question and question still;
"Had her dear likeness smiled on high,
    "I might have gazed my fill.

"Dreaming that life within the eye
    "Was kindling more and more,
"I could have sat for ever by
    "Her shadow on the floor.

" And if my spirit lacking strength
    " Felt desolate and sad,
" I could have watched her, till at length
    " Her looks had made me glad.

" Oh tell me, tell me, Nurse, to-night,
    " Was she not mild and fair?
" Which were the rooms of her delight,
    " What garments did she wear?"

" Your mother, sweet," the nurse replies,
    " Indeed was wondrous fair;
" Like yours her dove-like hazel eyes,
    " Like yours her auburn hair.

" In that same room, she loved the best,
    " You sleep, my child, each night;
" And like an angel, she was drest,
    " Ever in raiment white.

" But these are stories for the day,
    " When summer sunbeams fall,
" With searching and enlivening ray
    " Around this wild old hall.

" Suffer not now such thoughts of pain
    " About your heart to stay,
" Or the dim workings of the brain
    " Will chase all sleep away."

Still feeling on her orphaned breast
    A weight of tender gloom,
She reached the chamber of her rest,
    Her mother's favourite room;

And sinking with a quiet sigh
    Into the offered chair,
She scarcely felt the nurse untie
    Her waving auburn hair.

Within that consecrated space,
    You could not but have felt,
Touched by the spirit of the place,
    That THERE a Virgin dwelt.

There seemed a presence half divine
    Floating unseen above—
The shadow of calm thoughts, the sign
    Of maiden faith, and love;

As if her spotless heart had shed
    A dew of pureness there,
Which brooded o'er the placid bed,
    And glorified the air.

Beautiful Agnes! sitting still
    Before a mirror tall,
Letting the auburn curls at will
    On her white shoulder fall.

She gazed into the solemn skies,
   Now hung with boundless night;
Her large uplifted hazel eyes
   Floating in liquid light;

Whilst from her fresh and lucent skin
   A lustre seemed to pour,
Like delicate pink tints, within
   Shells from an Indian shore.

In pensive silence thus the maid
   Her loveliness undrest;
The nurse in silence gave her aid,
   Then left her to her rest.

The silver lamp was quenched in gloom,
   The prayer was duly said,
And the dim quiet of the room
   Closed o'er her graceful head.

Beautiful Agnes! may she sleep
   Until the golden day,
Beneath an angel's wing, to keep
   All evil things away.

But soft—she wakes, as if in fear;
   What sights or sounds invade
The wavering eye—or dreaming ear,
   To make her thus afraid?

The nurse was summoned to her side.
    "Is then my darling ill?"
"No, but the lamp, dear nurse," she cried;
    "You left it burning still."

"Nay, look, my love, no lamp is near,
    "The room was black as night;
"This taper I have carried here—
    "There is no other light."

"Have I then roused you up in vain?
    "I must have dreamt," she said;
And on the silken couch again
    Down dropped her flower-like head.

But, on the closing of the door,
    Again the room was bright;
O'er cornice, curtain, ceiling, floor,
    Fluttered that wondrous light.

High o'er her pillow, she beheld
    A glory gliding nigher,
From which, as from a fountain, welled
    Floods of innocuous fire;

And in the middle of the light
    A wingèd woman there,
With hazel eyes, and raiment white,
    And waving auburn hair.

Upon the silent girl below
  Her looks of beauty fell,
Speaking of peace earth cannot know,
  And love ineffable.

And Agnes gazed a little while,
  Then prayed for strength and grace,
Till both came issuing from the smile
  Upon that woman's face.

Whether in words, to human sense,
  The spirit found its way,
Or by some mystic influence,
  The maiden could not say.

But words, or thoughts, an angel sway
  Lived on her heart like balm,
So that her senses, as she lay,
  Were steeped in wondrous calm.

And thus, a heaven-sent messenger,
  Upon her human child,
Scarcely more beautiful than her,
  The spirit-mother smiled.

Mother and daughter felt through death
  Their hearts grow one in love;
Delicious human tears beneath,
  And seraph smiles above.

And then the Aspect told the maid,
  By word, or look, or sign,
That she must pass from earthly shade
  Into a light divine:

That it had pleased the Lord to give
  Them both a precious boon,
And that her child should come to live
  With her to-morrow noon.

When this was said, the air grew dim
  And Agnes felt her brain
Down a bright stream of vision swim,
  To slumbrous depths again.

Oh! there was trouble in the hall
  When Agnes told her tale,
A shadow of strange fear on all—
  She only did not quail.

She only said, "This wondrous show,
  "Though true and clear it seem,
" By my own reason taught, I know
  "May only be a dream.

" And if a dream it be, why soon
  " The cloud it leaves is gone;
" But if a spirit—then at noon,
  " God's holy will be done."

Then grave physicians came, to try
    If fever lurked within
The splendours of the hazel eye,
    Or the translucent skin.

But nothing they could find, to show
    One trace of feverish heat;
As soft and calm as falling snow,
    Her maiden pulses beat.

"Cool is her blood," they said; "unriven
    "The peaceful nerves and brain;
"Our skill is idle—and with Heaven
    "The issue must remain.

"Let her go forth to usual things,
    "The tasks of every day,
"Until this dream, which round her clings,
    "Dies silently away."

Pensively then the maiden's eye
    Turned to the climbing sun;
But ever, as the hour went by,
    Its usual task was done,

Until that sun had ceased to climb
    The fathomless mid-heaven,
And noon was drawing near, the time
    To holy music given.

Her minstrel did not come; and tired
    With waiting on so long,
She sat her down, like one inspired,
    And poured her soul in song.

    "Christe, miserere mei,
        "Praebe, Mater, lucem,
    "Miserere, Agne Dei,
        "Per eternam crucem."

The Minstrel, stealing in alone,
    Stood tranced beside the door;
"For sounds came forth," he said, "unknown,
    "Except in Heaven, before."

And often he was wont to say,
    And to that faith did cling,
That He, who listened on that day,
    Had heard an angel sing.

At once the song stops hurriedly,
    As if without her will;
Though floods of viewless melody
    Seem eddying round her still.

Gracefully then the maiden bent
    Over her throbbing lute,
As if to sweep the strings she meant;
    But still those strings were mute.

The dial points to noon—and hark!
  The old clock shakes its tower;
Yet, strange to say, she did not mark
  The coming of that hour.

A sunbeam touched her placid brow,
  If earthly beam it were,
And tinted with a golden glow
  Her trembling auburn hair.

She stirred not—and it seemed to lie
  A glory on her head;
But when that splendour had passed by,
  They found—that she was dead!

So gentle was her death—so blest—
  Under the covering cross,
That even those who loved her best
  Could scarcely mourn their loss.

They laid her, Heaven's selected bride,
  Her mother's grave within—
Two sainted sleepers, side by side,
  Far from the strife of sin.

Beautiful Agnes! may she sleep
  Thus, till the Judgment day,
Beneath an angel's wing, to keep
  All evil things away.

TO TWO SISTER BRIDES.[1]

WHO WERE MARRIED ON THE SAME DAY.

Not surely to unmixed delight,
  Not to unhesitating mirth,
These trembling veils of virgin white
  And bridal orange-flowers give birth.

In the same cradle ye have slept
  The sleep that only childhood may,
Together smiled, together wept,
  Together knelt, and learned to pray.

Together!—in that solemn word
  What depth of love, what meaning lies!
It is as if the heart were stirred
  By angel hymns from Paradise.

And now these twin-like years are o'er,
  These clasping tendrils disentwined,
Your thoughts and hopes can flow no more
  As channeled in a single mind.

[1] Mrs. Gladstone, and Mary Glynne, the first wife of George Lord Lyttelton.

TO TWO SISTER BRIDES.

Behind you, shifting rapidly
   Like the wild rack before the blast,
In mazy movement, flutter by
   The dream-like tissues of the past.

Before you, full of mystery,
   Ages unborn their shadows fling;
Time, with its seed eternity,
   Sleeps in each slender marriage ring.

What marvel, then, that as ye kneel
   There fall some consecrating tears,
That dizzily ye seem to feel
   The motion of the moving spheres?

But though dim shapes the air may fill,
   One spot of heaven smiles above,
Through which, with lustre calm and still,
   Shines on your hearts the star of love.

And wider yet, from day to day
   That stainless spot on high shall spread;
And yet more full, love's living ray,
   Cover with light each graceful head.

Cold were the man whose eyes could rest
   On this beloved and lovely pair,
Nor feel within his thrilling breast,
   A gush of blessing and of prayer.

TO TWO SISTER BRIDES.

Ay, colder than the sunless north—
    Than the frore gale that numbs the sea—
The heart that is not rushing forth,
    Like brooks, by sudden spring set free.

Not such the multitudes, who press
    To look upon you once again,
In reverential tenderness,
    And tears, half pleasure and half pain.

Oh, priceless tribute! these are they
    Whose lives were soothed and raised by you;
On whom your gentle presence lay,
    As upon flowers the evening dew

Their loss they know, yet it is borne
    Without a touch of selfish fear;
Albeit, as if the spring were torn
    For ever from the rolling year.

Not human hearts alone—the skies—
    (Nor over dark, nor over bright),
Are clad in mystic sympathies,
    Of tender gloom, and chastened light.

So mild the sun, so soft the gray,
    It almost seems as if there were
A spirit in the silent day—
    A feeling on the lifeless air:

As if these lawns and woodlands, full
   Of a deep instinct, resting not,
Motioned away the beautiful,
   In loving sadness to their lot.

Yes—and for both that lot shall glow
   With splendours, not the gift of time;
Keeping undimmed, through weal and woe,
   The promise of its maiden prime.

High hopes are thine, oh! eldest flower,
   Great duties to be greatly done;
To soothe, in many a toil-worn hour,
   The noble heart which thou hast won.

Covet not then the rest of those,
   Who sleep through life unknown to fame;
Fate grants not passionless repose
   To her, who weds a glorious name.

He presses on through calm and storm
   Unshaken, let what will betide;
Thou hast an office to perform,
   To be his answering spirit bride.

The path appointed for his feet
   Through desert wilds and rocks may go,
Where the eye looks in vain to greet
   The gales, that from the waters blow.

TO TWO SISTER BRIDES.

Be thou a balmy breeze to him,
    A fountain singing at his side;
A star, whose light is never dim,
    A pillar, through the waste to guide.

Nay, haply, not of thee alone
    This proud futurity is true;
Wreaths, on as green a laurel grown,
    To thy bright sister may be due.

Your happy destiny has been
    To find another tie in them,
Where others might have rushed between
    The sister roses on the stem.

Like double stars, the even beam
    Of their young glory burns on you;
So that the nearer heart may deem
    Her own the brighter of the two.

Let this yet more your souls unite,
    Into one woven thought and will;
Reflecting, like twin mirrors, light
    And beauty on each other still.

THE POETASTER'S PLEA.

A FAMILIAR EPISTLE TO W. E. GLADSTONE, ESQ. M.P.,
WRITTEN MANY YEARS AGO.

ONE of a long-oppressed insulted crew,
At length, dear Gladstone, I appeal to you!
I do not mean the warrior of the state,
Clothed in bright armour at the temple's gate:
Set in the front of battle, to uphold
The truth that streams in glory from of old;
To praise thy bearing in that arduous fight,
Proud friends, and unresentful foes unite;
And the hushed spirits of the future see
Even now, a lord of human kind in thee.
Not to the man or statesman, now I speak;
Another, who is yet the same, I seek,—
One of a joyous company, who hied
Through the green fields along the river side,
Those laughing fields, which wear for you and me
A garment of perpetual youth and glee,
Where voices call us, that are heard no more,
And our "lost Pleiad" brightens as before.

To one I turn—the monarch of debate,
President Minos of our little state,
Who, when we met to give the world the law
About Confucius, Cæsar, or Jack Straw,
Saw with grave face the unremitting flow
Of puffs and jellies from the shop below;
At the right moment, called us to forsake
Intrusive fruit, and unattending cake;
And if unheeded, on the stroke of four,
With rigid hand closed the still-opening door,
Denouncing ever after in a trice,
That heinous breach of privilege—an ice—
To one, who in his editorial den
Clenched grimly an eradicating pen,
Confronting frantic poets with calm eye,
And dooming hardened metaphors to die.
Who, if he found his young adherents fail,
The ode unfinished, uncommenced the tale,
With the next number bawling to be fed,
And its false feeders latitant or fled,
Sat down unflinchingly to write it all,
And kept the staggering project from a fall.
Nor men, nor gods, nor yet the trade, alas!
Will license middling poetry to pass;
So Horace tells us, but is Horace right?
I own I think his dictum merely spite.
The pampered favourite only means to say
That Roman Grub-streets bored his soul away,
Ecstatic bards beset his path in swarms,

And Bavius clasped him in fraternal arms.
Hoarse Mævius talked his best to make him stare,
Whilst he sat shuddering in his elbow chair;
Hence, full of bile, he raised his arm on high,
And smote that hapless legion, hip and thigh.
Succeeding times have echoed on the strain,
And spent their fury on the tribe, in vain:
In self-conceit invulnerably mailed,
We stand, however savagely assailed,
And pour into the drowsy ear of time
Our never ebbing tides of blank and rhyme.
Coxcombs there are, no doubt, by scribbling made,
Sons of a shapeless star—for every shade
Of many-coloured life alike unfit—
Who deem themselves the miracles of wit.
Through all the forms of our great art they crawl,
Producing nothing, but infesting all;
To some mysterious wisdom make pretence,
Sneer at plain strength of head, and stalwart sense;
Discover then that rhyme is not a knife,
To open at their will, the oyster—life;
Grow sour and bitter, and fermenting fast
Fret into eager vinegar at last,
Till the vexed world wraps, in one general curse,
Each luckless vagabond who writes a verse.
Still, setting these aside, a whining few,
Why loose your dogs against our harmless crew?
At my own cost I give the world my own—
It does not please you? leave it then alone.

To the dull page no law chains down your eye;
No act of parliament compels to buy;
No general warrant do I hold, to keep
Members from their diurnal prose and sleep,
Squires from the Derby, lawyers from the courts,
Or you, from those seducing blue reports,
Where Elliot[1] does his best stale fish to cry,
And Lin[2] to blacken the Barbarian Eye.
What, though a thousand holders of the quill
Can write as well, or better if you will?
What, though I never hope to see my rhyme
Surmount one ripple of the stream of time?
Why should I stay my hand? or blot what lends
A touch of pleasure to some partial friends,
Whilst praise and fame, in every grade belong
Unto the sister arts—design and song?
Freely we grant our talents are but small,
But is it better to have none at all?
Unridiculed by men or gods, we see
A sketcher, sitting under every tree:
Not theirs the hands, that can express at will,
Gigantic visions with unerring skill.
No mighty genius moulds the vast design,
No labouring thought inheres in every line;
Near the rapt eye, as still the shapes they trace,
There floats no mild unfathomable face,

---

[1] Our minister in China at the time.
[2] The Chinese commissioner at Canton, thought by many to write better despatches than his European antagonists.

Whose human beauty melts into seraphic grace.
Still, praised themselves, they teach us to admire
The depth which awes, the models that inspire;
Were there none such (like gradual hills set high
To parley with the peaks that drink the sky),
Apelles might have lived and died unknown,
And Phidias left unshaped the Parian stone.
So, but for us, a scorned, a trampled throng,
Homage would fail the sacred kings of song;
Did not our spirits catch the dawning blaze,
Reflect the glory, and transmit the rays,
Beams of the sun without an atmosphere,
Great poets would be useless aliens here.
If still you shake your head, I can but say,
That thus I smoothe the roughness of the way.
At Eton taught to bear, and to forbear,
I boast of no magnificent despair;
I am not good, or bad, enough to know
The isolation of especial woe;
Still there are times, when fever and unrest
Besiege the silent fortress of the breast;
Unspoken heaviness and cares unshown,
Which yet are bitter to endure alone;
When on some sunny dream cloud-shadows fall,
Or sorrows come to me that come to all—
Days of uprooted hope—of fading flowers—
Of rainbows, waning into wintry showers—
When hidden languor follows secret strife,
And the heart sickens at the length of life—

THE POETASTER'S PLEA.

These are the seasons, which of right belong
To thoughts, which rush and kindle into song.
No idle dream of fame, no servile fear
Of the world's scorn, beset and goad me here.
Instinctively, my shattered spirits come
To look for peace within their natural home;
In that small circle still, defying fate,
I can at least, or well or ill, create,
Till genial art has charmed away the pain,
And the soul strengthens to her work again.
The humblest thus appear to draw more nigh
To the great heirs of immortality—
Milton rose up when fate grew hard to bear,
From earth to Heaven, and drew empyrean air.
From the salt bread he loathed, and paths of pain,
Up alien stairs, when life was on the wane,
The Tuscan sought his seraph love again.
And Tasso kept in gloom, when hope was dead,
One brightness, from the laurel on his head.
Auguster grief was theirs, whose awful sound,
Sea-like, is heard the listening earth around—
But yet the same perennial fountains fill
The ocean-deeps, and shallows of the rill.
Though vast the space between us, not the less
We seek a common solace in distress.
Enough of this—and kindly take from me
These fragments as a poetaster's plea.

THE HYPERBOREAN MAIDEN.

"These Hyperborean virgins died in Delos . . . Their sepulchre is on the left hand, within a spot consecrated to Diana, and covered by an olive tree."—HERODOTUS.

SCYTHIAN.

WHAT does this olive here?

DELIAN PRIEST.

Its branches weave a holy gloom,
Over the northern maiden's tomb,
    Throughout the year;
She came from a land that is far away,
Where the brightness of our southern day
    Is all unknown,
To listen to our Delian god;
And here, beneath the flowery sod,
    She sleeps alone.
And this olive rose up silently,
To shade with its sacred canopy
    Her quiet sleep:
And our Delian virgins every year,
With solemn music come, and here
    Bend down to weep;

Whilst all the flowers of Greece are shed
Above the Scythian damsel's head.

SCYTHIAN.

It is not beneath the olive shade,
That a northern maiden should be laid,
    Deep though it be,
Nor near these marble halls of pride,
With stifling incense flooded wide;
    Her spirit free
Should dwell, where the cool breeze at even
Brings whispers of her native heaven.
And your god should have called a stately tree,
From the forests that frown o'er the northern sea,
    Her tomb to shade:
He should have called a mighty pine,
With gnarlèd boughs, and knotted rind,
To catch the wailings of the wind,
    Where she is laid:
For the olive, and the purple vine,
Though bright in the sun their green leaves shine,
    Know not the maid;
But the solemn tree of the north would spread
Its shadow in love o'er her narrow bed;
And the breath of the simple flowers that blow
At the melting of the northern snow,
Would lend delight to the visions of death,
When she dreameth silently beneath.

THE ATHENIAN BATTLE-HYMN
AT MARATHON.

The beginning and end of this composition are to be taken as the inherited battle-hymn of the Ionian race; of that branch of it, at least, which was seated in Attica. In the middle I have added some lines, pointing to the particular emergency; there was, I apprehend, no such addition in point of fact; but I think myself justified poetically in supposing it to have been made, considering the terror of the Athenians, and the unusual importance of the crisis.

ONCE more a threatening trumpet
   Across our skies is borne;
Once more, a foeman's footstep
   Tramples Ionian corn.
In thy stern Father's shining hall,
   Pallas Athenè, hear,
Be thou to us a brazen wall,
   Be thou our shield and spear;
Ionian goddess undefiled,
Unmothered and unwedded child
   Of the Eternal name,
When we call upon thee, hear us,
In the mist of strife be near us,

Be a strong arm, to uprear us
   From the gulfs of death and shame
Be a keen unwaning star,
   With threatening might
   Of arrowy light,
Piercing the cloud of hostile war.
With them are alien gods—be *thou*
Among us, and about us, now.

Down from thy Father's shining hall,
   With meteor swiftness leap,
Unconquered, hear us when we call,
   Thy people's needs are deep;
No common perils round us hover,
   No common foes have vowed
Our temples and our homes to cover
   With ruin's earthquake cloud.

That baleful trumpet-note which passed
   Was waked by no Hellenic lips,
Those shadows on yon sea, are cast,
   Not from Corinthian ships.
Not now—along the river bank
   Careering wild and wide,
With lances set against our flank—
   Thessalian horsemen ride.
No Thracian drives his battle car
From black Pangæan heights afar,

Nor swelleth loud a Theban shout,
Nor Isle of Pelops poureth out
Her floods of Dorian war;
But hither from wild homes are rolled
The grim clans of the restless Mede,
Men, whom untravelled regions breed,
    And gods unknown uphold;
In yonder shining files have place
The Syrians of the iron mace,
The lords of the Cilician steed,
The Bactrian, with his bow of reed,
    The Paricanian spear,
The Arab shafts that never fail,
The scales of Persia's glittering mail,
The Sacian axe of giant force,
The lasso-armed Sagartian horse,
    And Libyan cars of fear.
Yet, though the Median lord be great,
Wanton in wealth, and drunk with hate,
Others, as mighty in estate,
Have fallen into cureless ill:
Yes, though the Median lord be great,
    Greater and mightier still
Are those, who pass through heaven's high gate,
    To work their Father's will;
Therefore in calmness we await
This travail of incumbent fate,
Because we know that thou canst smite
His myriads into headlong flight.

Now, ye shouts of men, go round,
Now, ye quickening trumpets, sound,
Now, each fife and clarion
Fling the battle-music on,
Fling forward, as a gathering flood,
The ancient melody of blood:
Like a beacon, let it dart
From lip to lip, from heart to heart,
   For great Athenè hears,
From rank to rank, from line to line,
She glides a spirit and a sign,
   Up with the old Ionian spears:
Hark! how her haughty footstep treads
Like living thunder o'er our heads,
Mark! where through æther's mystic veil
Burn glimpses of her gleaming mail;
The brazen shield is darkening o'er us,
The brazen lance is bright before us,
Ionian goddess! Maid divine,
We follow, where they move and shine.

ROBIN HOOD'S BAY.

THE NARRATIVE OF A REAL EVENT.

ADDRESSED TO THE ENGLISH PEOPLE.

Written in June 1878.

A. 1.

THE stream of Time runs wild and broken
Past rocks which moan and quiver,
And white waves, flashing past, betoken
A near fall in the river—
Swelled by black storms of fate and woe,
(As earthly streams from rain or snow),
With voice like thunder loud and deep,
The grim surge hovers on the steep,
Self-strengthening for its headlong leap
    To gulphs unseen below.
Soon from that shrouding gorge once more
To dash forth with exulting roar;
But who shall tell what may be done
Whilst it is hidden from the sun?
We only know, on looking back,
Along the pale Past's faded track,

That the world meets another clime
Below each cataract of Time:
New Dawn before, on realms fresh flowering;
Behind, Death's night its silence showering.

Proud England, can it be that thou,
Among lost Empire shadows in void space,
With a faint crown upon each frozen brow,
Art doomed at length to take thy Phantom place?
To the quenched stars that hail thee as a mate,
Low muttering in their ghostly speech, thy fortunes and thy fate—
Where is thy spirit's sword of flame?
Whose blade as lightning fell to smite
Fierce kings from triumph into shame,
Fierce kings that sought man's earth to blight
And trample into lifeless mire?
Where is thy people's heart of fire,
Before whose burning ray
The mighty soldier's sateless lust
Of blood and power was scorched away
And shrivelled into dust?
Was the Land's soul spent, filling Godlike men
With strength for that great task, that it might perish then?

A. 2.

Stung by such fears, alone I wandered
Past rocks a wild beach strewing,

And full of solemn sorrow pondered
On thoughts of shame and ruin :
The raw cliffs, with a moaning sound,
Shuddered in fragments to the ground ;
The cold sky crept on, thickening still
Above the terraced Raven hill ;
In each small bay the sea-mew shrill
Wheeled mournfully around ;
Whilst the long waves with sweeping flow,
Dead white above, gray lead below,
Plunged at the rocks that stretch away,
And seemed like ruthless beasts of prey
Devouring all before them—then
Laid low in sullen dreams agen.
No marvel, if my heart were drowned
In darkness, by these glooms around,
Like some faint guide's death-stricken taper,
That sinks in strangling cavern-vapour.

What was it then from earth or air,
(Like dawn that thrills with silent touches slow
The morning mist) stole through that bleak despair
Till darkness fled, light-conquered ; and the glow
Of vital warmth rose on my heart with power,
Like summer sunrise gathering life and strength
  from hour to hour ?
It seemed as if the dreaming earth
Below, the sky above us hung,
And the sea's tameless heart gave birth

To thoughts that spake without a tongue—
To old mysterious memories, stored
In heights and depths—and now out-poured
Whilst the land thrills all through,
Feeling blind forces, lent to her
By her dead sons till Time dies too,
  Within her bosom stir.
The strength of their proud instincts, living still,
Stream forth, as breathings old streamed through
  some sacred hill.

A. 3.

Thus, thus a life-scene of the Past,
On memory's magic mirror cast,
To the desponding heart was shown,
But not by memory alone;
For dim powers round were breathing in
A subtle spirit of their own.
Until the vision had up-grown,
Half from without, half from within:
As if the bitter hours between
With all their tears had never been,
And Time itself were quenched for me,
That I might feel and learn and see,
In spite of all which seems to sever,
That strong ties bind us still; that ever,
Clear as the stars and bold and free,
The bright rich blood of England runs
From heart to heart, through rich and poor, her
  daughters and her sons.

B. .I.

And so by second-sight, a second-sight,
Not of the future but from days gone by,
There moves before me, clad in silent light,
    A joyous company.
Round the grim points they stream, with rapid glance
Striving to pierce each tide-tossed pebble-heap,
And find if there among the flints—perchance—
    Onyx or agate sleep.
Still on they glide and hope at length to reach
That well-known ledge, where fossils never fail,
Hewn from the rock, or dropped upon the beach
    Out of the crumbling shale;
But the hours will not slacken in their pace,
Nor the wild sea pause on its destined way,
Because the loiterers in that lonely place
    Are thoughtless young and gay.
They do not mark how the wind beats on shore,
How sea-birds scream the driving gusts before,
And how the stealthy flood creeps onward more and more.

But in the street the fisher folk talk low,
Gather in knots, and hurry thence to learn
Where the bright girls have gone—for well they know
    The tide is on the turn.
Kindly but rough they come, and do not spare
To fling home truths at those who let them go,
"They're young," they say, "but you folk lounging there

"Are old enough to know
"That none on a strange coast should trust the tides,
"We must be quick as fire upon their track,
"For we shall need God's help, and luck besides,
       "To bring these wanderers back."
So they go forth, not thinking of themselves,
Make light of peril, clutch, and drag them home
'Neath shaken cliffs, and over wave-worn shelves,
       Through flood and breaking foam.
Still there was one too frail to hasten so,
From illness frail—and at each doubtful spot,
Her weak breath fluttered, and her steps fell slow—
       With a sea faltering not.
A sailor lad near her behind them staid;
With dauntless looks and words he cheered the maid:
"I will not leave you here," he cried; "be not afraid.

B. 2.

"Nay, lady, tremble not, but on each rock
"Plant your foot firmly, without haste or fear;
"A careless step, a slip, a sudden shock,
       "Might cost us both full dear."
So they passed on, until they reach at last
The knab[1] whose jagged fangs through biting spray
Grin fierce, and hold them both imprisoned fast
       Within a land-locked bay.
The billows raved upon it, and above

---

[1] Local word for projecting rocky point.

The foam leapt like a live thing sheet on sheet,
And ever drinking in that narrow cove,
    The waves played round their feet.
The boy's bold face fell for a moment then,
And he called out to some who watched on high,
"How runs the flood, and is there yet, my men,
    "A hope of getting by?"
But there was silence for a space among
That rough crowd, as if speech itself were wrong,
When words are winged with death; at length out of the throng
One answered, "Nay, my lad, 'tis now half tide."
Again he asked them, "If we cannot pass,
"Could we not climb?"—once more the voice replied,
    "Impossible—alas!"
Thus these two paused with Death about to strike,
But their brave hearts rose high, to meet the stroke,
And like the lightning flash, in both alike
    Their English impulse woke.
Those icy bars, that held their souls apart,
Melted at once before hot danger's breath,
As glaciers melt, when snow-clad mountains start
    Flame-shattered from beneath.
The boy's face flushed rose-red with noble pride:
"Keep a good heart," he softly said, "my dear,
"And lean on me; whatever may betide
    "I will not leave you here."
Keep a good heart, *my dear*—of name and blood
They recked not then: of wealth or social state;

The English boy and English girl there stood
    To meet an equal fate.
Brother and sister in the face of death,
The face of Him who all things levelleth,
Together twined they hung with intermingling breath.

B. 3.

The boy's strong arm upreared that maiden mild,
And clasped her close, as in an iron vice.
She, as they plunged into that water wild,
    Drew off her rings of price.
She mused, still clear amid that rush and whirl,
" If he be saved, whilst I am wrenched away,
" He shall not lose all memory of the girl
    " For whom he strove to-day.
" If yonder hungry surge our arms dislink,
" And drag me down into the cruel seas,
" I must try hard to keep the power to think
" And in his hand fix these."
Like a weed floating helpless in the flood,
She felt herself swung past the rock's harsh rim,
And they stood safe—he giving thanks to God,
    She praising God and him.
One heart beat in their breasts, as there they stood,
One spirit lightened from each noble face,
And made them kin, good, but not more than good
    Types of our English race.
Their lives were parted then, nor know I whether
Fate let them meet again on earth together,

Nor how in after years he rose or fell.
Not for itself the tale I tell,
Nor value that bold deed too much:
England has had full many a son
Like him; his act was only one
Among ten thousand such;
And many an English lady fair
Has steeled her soul to do and dare,
Before and since the vanished spring
When that young maiden armed her will
This deed high-hearted to fulfil—
Thought only, through the storm and stir,
Of one who risked his life for her,
And how with eye-balls drenched and dim,
She might, from fingers numb, for him
      Draw off each precious ring.
Not for itself the tale I tell:
But if, perchance, in this disastrous hour,
When gulphs are yawning wide as Hell
Between the rich and poor; when the grim power
Of hate is flushing like a poisonous flower
With evil blooms; and far and near
The hearts of men are failing them for fear—
If, in this lurid pause of Fate,
Whilst nations tremble as they wait;
The bringing back through Death—which then befell
That youthful pair can give us hope, can teach
How love is possible for all, and reach
The clouded heart of England—well!

C. 1.

Is there yet time, Oh Mother mine, to stanch
Those death-wounds ever dropping gore, which blanch
Thy fair large brows, and drain the heart away?
    Will God yet grant us time?
Oh, Mother, not to-morrow, but to-day,
Calm down those warring pulses, till thy brain
And heart forget long years of strife and pain,
Forget each jar of anguish, and regain
Their old harmonious chime.
For giant ships with iron clothed in vain,
And Islands armed along the Eastern sea,
Are but void dreams of power, unless there be
The spirit of the Past to throb and spread
Within those seeming strengths which else are dead.
If that worm Discord gnaw the root
Of England's old and stately tree,
Graces and gifts, like blighted fruit
From wasting boughs, will fall and lie
On the rank earth—fore-doomed to die.
Our proud wrath gathering stern and slow,
Our compacts woven close to throw
A bar before the unresting foe;
To say at length "No further shalt thou go:
"Here stay the trampling of those blood-stained feet,"
Are but as ropes of shivering sand,
Unless behind their lifeless framework beat
One heart and will—throughout the land.

C. 2.

This then be England's hope—her task—to fill
The gulph that parts her true sons, threatening still;
Let all men cast therein from either side,
With their whole mind and strength,
The evil thoughts and evil dreams which hide
The hearts of men from one another here—
Pale envy, sick distrust, and jealous fear—
Till the grim rifts brought nearer and more near
    May close in peace at length.
Then soon such golden memories as endear
The bygone years alike to all will rise
Out of the past, and fill the living skies
With visioned light, and instincts half divine,
That quench the hate of hostile orbs malign,
    Break up the sense of strangeness cold,
And teach us once again to prize
The kinship left, the links that hold,
The common blood and life which reach
To fountains of forgotten speech.
Whence the land's thousand tales once more
Shall stream through earth by every pore,
To warm all hearts from door to door,
Such as this legend haunting that gray shore,
Round which the German seas, loud-roaring, yet
Make perilous the wild path, where
The two beneath those staggering cliff-walls met
To leave a deathless memory there.

C. 3.

Surely the need is sore!
For not since Godwin's Harold rushed
To guard his native shore
Have men's expectant hearts been hushed
Into an awe more deep than now.
We know not when, or where, or how,
The tempest, ripening fast,
May break in wrath at last;
For still the lightning vapour threads
Each secret vein of Earth and Heaven:
One moment, and above our heads
The storm's heart may be riven,
With voice of mighty thunders, and
Fires answering from the deep, to melt away the land.

Then by each noble thought and deed,
Of every age, or class, or creed;
By all the generous lives poured forth
Against the anarch of the North;
By those bold hearts which never trembled
When India's myriads fierce assembled;
By the bright blood which sank like rain
Into the burning fields of Spain,
Or fattened Belgium's fatal plain;
By Nile's fierce struggle; by the stormlike cheers
That smote the Frenchman through the battle mist,
But faltered down to fitful murmurs, when
Strange sobs broke out among those iron men,

Whilst in that last pale triumph, full of tears,
Silent sad lips the dying hero kissed:[1]
Nor by such names to haughtiest honour known,
By glories speaking trumpet-tongued, alone:
But by each deed of love, from whence is drifted
A fresh life and a fragrance, such as cling
To the charmed wind, flower-melodies uplifted
Out of wild roses when they wake in spring;
By our great Past, seen or unseen, my brothers!
Since of such deeds some glow in light, whilst others
Though they die not, in darkness live,
Still are they our land's wealth, and not another's,
To her their spirit's heat they give,
Float through her deep heart everywhere,
Make rich our seas, and fill the air
With motions that forbid despair;
Known and unknown, we feel, are fused together
Into one soul of strength, and therefore, whether
They shine aloft like suns, or whether fall,
Blind silence round them and Oblivion's pall;
By their old Faith, old Love, old Fire, we call
On England, with her true sons, one and all,
To bid these jars, this sound of anger cease,
Until throughout our bounds be health and peace.

Thus from my heart its cloud of gloom I flung,
And went home cheered, along that rugged way
Whilst the pearl-tinted moon, slow-silvering, hung
Above the lonely Yorkshire bay.

[1] "Kiss me, Hardy," Nelson's last words.

THE UNOBTRUSIVE CHRISTIAN.

This portrait was suggested by the phrase of a friend that "my Christianity showed itself unobtrusively, perhaps too unobtrusively." At the same time it is a Fancy Portrait, and I do not mean to be identified with the ideal person in question, as, if I were, people might say that I treated Maurice, whom I regarded with the utmost reverence and affection, too lightly.

INTENT upon a Thankless Muse,
    From Youth to Age his course he ran,
Nor read he "Essays and Reviews,"
    That unobtrusive Christian man.

Sound as a Bishop's cob, he jogs
    Along the well-worn paths of yore—
Thinking dissenters vulgar dogs,
    And jawing Puseyites a bore.

Unvexed he saw Colenso blind
    His Zulu goats to Hell guide down:
On Maurice, who undamns mankind,
    He looked without or smile or frown.

THE UNOBTRUSIVE CHRISTIAN.

His creed no Parson ever knew,
  "For this was still his simple plan,"
To have with Clergymen to do
  As little as a Christian can.

He shirked their sermons, if he might,
  If not he crouched, and slept them through,
Half-hidden from revealing Light,
  A violet—planted in a pew.

STANZAS WRITTEN IN DEJECTION.

FROM THE CHINESE OF LI-TAI-PÉ.

This poet is considered by his countrymen, according to the Marquis d'Hervey St. Denys, their greatest poet. The admiration of the Chinese for him is so great that they have erected a temple in his honour, as the "Great Doctor," the "Prince of Poetry," and, what to European ears savours of bathos, "The Immortal given to Drink." He was born A.D. 702. He died at the age of 61, A.D. 763.

I.

The sun of yesterday which leaves me
   No earthly skill can woo to stay,
To-day's pale gloom which chills and grieves me
   No human arm can hold away :
The birds of passage, ever flying past,
In countless flocks stream down the autumn blast ;
I mount my tower to gaze far off, and fast
   Fill wine-cups from the waning jar.

II.

The mighty bards, long dead, seem rising
   Around me in this lonely place ;

I murmur through the old songs, prizing
   Their matchless vigour, truth, and grace.
I too feel powers that will not be controlled,
But cannot rival here the great of old,
Till to pure skies up-soaring, I behold,
   More closely, each unclouded star.

III.

Vainly our swords would cleave the river:
   It keeps its ever-living flow;
Vainly in wine-cups, mantling ever,
   We strive to drown the sense of woe—
Man, in this life, when stormy fate grows dark,
Must let her billows rock his wandering bark,
Give the wild waves their will, nor pause to mark
   Too keenly how they foam afar.

THE NIGHT AND THE DAY.

THEY met in the hour of the dim twilight,
The hour that is neither day nor night;
Like two proud queens, they met on high,
In that neutral space of the summer sky,
Where the evening star, when the day is done,
Shines through the haze of the sunken sun.
    The first was darkly pale—with eyes
    Deeper than are the midnight skies,
    Pale as an Indian monarch's bride,
    The burning pyre beside;
    Yet lovely as the seraphim,
    When pitying tears their splendour dim;
    Tears shed in heaven itself, to see
    The depth of human misery:
    Her voice was musical, and low;
    With something in its tone
    Of charmèd power, that seemed to flow
    From worlds to man unknown.
    Beneath her broad imperial brow,
    Those deep eyes darkly shone,

Pure as the wreathèd stars below,
That glowed within her burning zone.
The second was a brighter maiden:
Her brow with curls of gold was laden;
Her smile was sparkling, clear, and free,
Though stately as a queen was she.
Her jewelled neck and arms were bare,
Snow-white, beneath her sunny hair—
Each vein was filled with fire, and lent
Her eye ethereal merriment;
Upon her cheek there lived a blush,
Warm as the sunset's tender flush;
A tone in her glad voice had she,
At which the heart beat like the sea,
When the west wind bloweth warm and free,
And a merry glance, like the smile of Spring,
Which made each pulse a living thing.
But her dark rival stood, sedate,
With soothing eyes compassionate,
Whose light my very heart did fill
With visions that subdued the will,
And bowed me with a sudden sense
Of unresisted reverence;
For by the brow, divinely fraught
With incommunicable thought—
By those low tones, which seemed to be
The accents of eternity—
By all the living memories
Shrined in those calm and searchless eyes,

It was as though no voice had told,
As though no seraph could unfold
The mighty mysteries that sleep,
In that still spirit hidden deep.
Then, as the blue-eyed maiden bent
Above her charmèd instrument,
And breathed unto the listening air
Strains sweet enough to lull despair,
Those eyes of beauty did express
A pure and pitying tenderness,
And on her lip there gleamed the while
A calm and melancholy smile.

THE DAY.

I am the queen of earth and sea;
Who shall dispute the palm with me?
I am lovely as of yore,
When, upon the clouded shore
Of an abysmal sea, I stood,
Enkindled by the breath of God.
All things then that hate the light—
All the gloomy brood of Night,
Fled before me, as I blest
The raging deep with peace, and rest.
Then—the proud giant of the sun
Leapt forth his glorious race to run,
And the breathing world her course begun;
How beautiful it was, to see
Beneath *my* beams, all things that be

Awake in primal revelry !
Oh turn to me from the dark dull Night,
For my voice is the voice of life and light !

THE NIGHT.

Mine is the sceptre of the sky,
And mine the starry worlds on high :
   Those fountains of eternal light,
Which feed the immeasurable void
With life and splendour undestroyed,
   And tell that God is infinite.
Thou knowest how the midnight sky
Fills the weak heart with purity;
How all the dreams of wrath and sin,
That lurk the soul's lone caves within,
To make its peace their prey—take flight
Before the blessèd breath of Night.
Thou know'st the reverential sense
Of God and His omnipotence;
The tears of pleasantness that rise
"Up from the heart into the eyes"—
Thou know'st the sweet and solemn fear,
As if the holy dead were near,
And the deep touch of earthly love,
When the stars are shining bright above,
And all things that about us lie
Inhale *their* immortality.
   If these have charms to move thee,
   Follow and love me.

THE DAY.

Bring all the flowers beneath the sun,
That shut their leaves when the light is gone—
For mine is the breath of the crimson rose,
Mine is every bud that blows;
Oh turn from the dark dull Night to me,
For mine is the beauty of earth and sea!
Thy spirit shall be clear as day,
Thy smile shall be the morning ray,
Whose light, wherever it may fall,
Sheds love and blessedness o'er all.
Thy soul shall feel the soft caress
Of unimagined happiness;
For all the roses that combine
To veil the ills of life, are mine:
Mine are the crowded cities, where
Mirth is always on the air—
Where no shadow can eclipse
The smile that lives upon the lips,
But all things ever seem to be
Steeped in sunny revelry.
Mine is the joyous wine-cup, bright
And burning with imprisoned light;
Mine are the melodies which fill
The heart with a voluptuous thrill,
Which cloud the spirit with excess
Of most tumultuous happiness,
And drown all sense of pain in man,

As fully as the wine-cup can.
Mine are the maidens of sunny hair,
   And eyes divinely blue;
Mine is the love that knows no care,
   But yet is warm and true.
O turn to me from the gloomy Night,
For my voice is the voice of life and light!

THE NIGHT.

Many a cycle has there been,
With gulfs of nothingness between;
Many a time have life and birth
Revisited the agèd earth:
Learn, mortal, that to me alone,
The secret things of the past are known;
Mine is every charmèd rhyme,
Freighted with spells of ancient time,
Strains divinely sweet, which sing
The deeds of many a giant king,
Whose life was mighty in each limb,
Whose soul was as the seraphim.
I can place before thine eye
The mirror of eternity;
I can show thee imaged there
Shadows of all things that were,
And bid Oblivion's self unfold
The treasures of his cavern old:
Stately cities ever bright
With porphyry, and chrysolite;

And wild primeval things, that sleep
Low-buried in the purple deep.
Mine are all the ruins gray
Which, since their prime has passed away,
Are garmented, to Fancy's sight,
In the still beauty of the Night:
Mine is Babylon the great,
Mine her river desolate,
And that sky-cleaving citadel,
Above the golden halls of Bel:
Mine are the towers along the Nile
Where Power and Wisdom dwelt erewhile—
The labyrinths, whose courts enfold
The melancholy gods of old—
The obelisks, unfallen still,
On some lone Abyssinian hill,
Covered with uncouth shapes, which brood
Above the lion-haunted wood.
Hers is this world of life and breath,
But *mine* the treasuries of death;
All things holy and divine
Whose light on earth has ceased to shine,
High hopes and visions that are fled,
Pure feelings that have perishèd—
Deep love whose passionate caress
Grew still more tender in distress—
And all the genius of the dead
Which never can be rivallèd.
Mine is the music pure and deep,

Such as poets hear in sleep,
Where Genius, clear as heaven above,
And quickened by intensest love,
Dreams of the beautiful and true,
Such as the cold world never knew,
And feeling soft as morning dew,
Unite, like streams upon the lea,
Into one simple melody:
Mine are the maidens who delight
With tender loveliness, like Night,
With voices of a thrilling sound
That shed the peace of Love around,
And pensive feelings deep, that shine
Through spiritual eyes divine.
   If these have charms to move thee,
   Follow and love me.
I covet not the incense blind,
The mad allegiance of mankind—
How should I, born the ancient queen
Of all beyond this narrow scene?
My kingdom knows nor time nor place,
It is the lone abyss of space—
The illimitable darkness thrown
Round petty systems, like a zone;
Still, though above the touch of woe,
I pity those who weep below.
As I sit, crowned with power, alone
Upon my everlasting throne,
I feel that the gloom around is rife

With the spirit of enduring life,
And cherish amid darkness dull
The image of the beautiful.
A thousand times has the light of Day
Startled those holy dreams away;
A thousand times has the brute mass
Felt God's eternal pinions pass
Through the gross element, that holds
Pale Chaos in her cumbrous folds:
I have seen it waken every time,
To be the theatre of crime.
I have seen sick dreams of fancied good,
As life and happiness pursued,
And the blessed hopes that cannot die
Again and again passed idly by.
I am wearied out at length to see
The same vain toil repeatedly—
The self-deceit, the ceaseless strife,
The utter vanity of life.
Her promised joys will end once more,
In gloom and sorrow, as of yore.
I am *very* weary of the past,
Oh take the peace I bring at last!

She ceased to speak, but my charmèd soul
Bowed down before her soft control;
And I left the Day, with her flaunting light,
To follow the calm and starry Night.

THE MOTHER AND DAUGHTER.

"And she, being before instructed of her mother, said, Give me here John Baptist's head in a charger."—MATTHEW xiv. 8.

In yon proud chamber, cool and still,
    The maid and mother meet—
Whilst yet the dance's joyous thrill
    Throbs in those fairy feet.
The damsel prattles, as a bird
    In April sunshine sings;
But scarcely half her tale was heard,
    When up that mother springs—

"No, child, I was not there to see;
    "But is he thus well pleased?
"And hath he bound himself to thee?
    "Why, then my soul is eased.
"The emerald brooch, the opal ring,
    "Ask of some other hand;
"To clench the promise of a king,
    "What kings can give, demand.

"Let Time to come send gems and gold,—
 "On whispering love they wait;
"This precious hour is mine, I hold
 "And claim it all, for hate.
"A head which God, forsooth, hath sown
 "With seeds of power and light,
"Is costlier, sure, than any stone,—
 "We'll have that head to-night.

"What! faint and white? what, dost thou dare
 "To gasp a girlish 'No?'
"Is, then, thy spirit light as air,
 "Thy blood but coloured snow?
"Off with that wan, imploring face,
 "Those arms which hang round me,
"Like the false growth, whose mock embrace
 "But kills its nurturing tree.

"The venom of the man I hate
 "Fell on us both alike;
"Kind Heaven hath armed thy hand with fate,
 "And yet thou wilt not strike.
"Why, then with idle words have done,
 "Keep idler tears aloof,
"And waste not shows of love on one
 "Who seeks a single proof.

"Lo! from its secret shrine I bring
 "This vessel rich and rare;

" Kept sacred from each meaner thing,
   " A prophet's head to bear.
" To yon crowned dastard speed like fire,
   " Who knows not what he swore ;
" Wring from that oath my soul's desire,
   " Or see my face no more."

The maid had come, in maiden mirth,
   To greet that mother mild ;
Whose tenderness, e'en from her birth,
   Had never failed the child.
Can this be she, with fevered breath,
   Which blood alone can slake,
Whose triumph, in that glance of death,
   Sits like the hooded snake ?

Forth shot, from her electric eye,
   Through each young vein a chill,
Palsying the heart, and freezing dry
   The fountains of the will.
The very sense of self grew numb,
   As by some spell destroyed,
Whilst alien thoughts unslackening come
   To throng the dreamlike void.

Against their rushing floods of strength
   The soul that seemed her own,
Like a spent swimmer, droops at length,
   Engulfed and overthrown ;

And still, to every sobbing prayer,
    The savage face she met
Glared, in its gloomy rancour there,
    More overmastering yet.

Then died of her despair the cry,
    The wail of her remorse,
Beat down unheard, and silenced by
    The stormier passion's force.
So fitful gusts, whose shuddering moan
    Before the tempest creeps,
Are crushed and quenched, whilst from his throne
    The conquering thunder leaps.

The charger to her head rose slow,
    Embossed with golden flowers;
And, with a step that seemed to go
    Rolled on by outward powers,
She glided, ghost-like, from the hall,
    Into the twilight gray;
As noiseless as the stars that fall,
    Glide into gloom away.

The woman watched with haughty sneer,
    Till, all at once, the roar
Of the long revel sounding near,
    Sunk down, and rose no more.
"That silence speaks," she murmured then;
    "The toils are round thee now;

"Too weak to have it said of men
"That Herod breaks his vow."

Then, pressing down her deep desire,
    She strode across the room;
The shuttle, from her touch of fire,
    Hissed through the shivering loom.
That steady hand, that eye of power,
    Worked fiercely firm and true;
Leaf after leaf, each woven flower,
    Beneath her fingers grew.

Tumult arose, with anger blent,
    She did not seem to heed;
But toiled like one whose hours hard spent
    Can just her children feed.
Faint steps at length were heard to beat,
    Chilled arms around her clung;
And, reddening those remorseless feet
    The loaded charger rung.

The woman raised her ghastly prize,
    Looked long, but looked in vain,
To find, within those placid eyes,
    Some trace of fear or pain.
Warm, on the milk-white marble floor,
    Broad drops of crimson fell;
She watched them curdle into gore,
    And coldly said, "'Tis well!"

Men left their fields half tilled, next morn,
    Half pruned their spreading vines;
To lift in prayer their hands forlorn,
    And weary Heaven for signs.
It seemed as if the Lord of Hosts
    No longer cared to reign;
Whilst Israel mourned, throughout her coasts,
    That more than prophet slain.

IN MEMORIAM.

(MAJOR STEUART SMITH.)

I.

THERE sweeps across the ocean foam
    A chill blast, heavy with despair,
And many a broken English home
    Is shuddering into silent prayer;
Unlooked for and undreamt of, strike
    Those words of evil, wounding deep,
To rouse us wild with terror, like
    The stab that murders sleep.

II.

Yet in the ruin death and shame
    In the dark rush of howling crowds,
(Like a star evermore the same
    Above all tempest-shaken clouds,)
Shines forth a brave soul, to be known
    Through the long ages as they run;
He, who of England thought alone,
    And surely spiked the gun.

III.

When that strange earthquake of defeat,
    That storm of horrible surprise,
Upon our weary soldiers beat,
    He would not even lift his eyes;
Through all the slaughter raging wide,
    He saw a duty to be done,
With time to do it, ere he died,—
    And so he spiked the gun.

IV.

Happier than his brave comrades then,
    He kept a clear unwavering will;
They could but fight and fall like men,
    But he worked hard for England still:
His last sad strokes rang firm and true,
    And his whole heart was filled with one
Proud thought to sweeten death—*he knew*
    That he had spiked the gun.

V.

Luxurious weaklings murmur low,
    Because they think the road is rough:
"Are lives worth having—Aye or No?"
    We find this answer good enough:
Yes, it is well that we should live,
    Though lampless be man's path and dim,
If life at honour's call can give
    A strength to die like him.

VI.

For him at least Death crowns; we send
    Two men to do the work of five;
Then, if they fail us, turn and rend
    The one who may be left alive.
Nay, if both fall, at both we chafe,
    In our mean anger sparing none:
Still, he from evil tongues is safe—
    The man who spiked the gun.

VII.

Let loose your sorrow without fear,
    Ye who now proudly mourn the dead;
No wind of bitterness can sear
    The oakleaves[1] round that sacred head.
A wave on glory's living sea,
    Till Fate's cold grasp hath quenched the sun—
Arrayed in light the name shall be
    Of him who spiked the gun.

[1] The civic crown—ob cives servatos.

SONNET TO HELEN,

ON THE OCCASION OF SENDING HER A TRIFLING PRESENT.

A MOMENTARY wish passed through my brain,
    To be the monarch of a magic place
Thick sown with burning gems, or to constrain
    The uncouth help of some half-demon race,
Vexing the pearl-paved hollows of the main
    For thee, and starry caverns in far space:
It was a wish unwisely formed, and vain;
    Even in the humblest trifles, love can trace
That which no mine can give, no Ariel's wing
From depths beneath or heights above can bring;
The memories of each kind look and tone,
    Gestures, and glancing smiles, into the gift
    Pass like a living spirit, and uplift
Its value, to the level of their own.

TO AN OLD COAT.

(FROM BÉRANGER.)

Poor coat, well loved for many reasons,
    Since both of us grow old, Be true;
This hand has brushed you for ten seasons,
    E'en Socrates no more could do.
Whilst Time your thin and white-seamed stuff
    Keeps on attacking without end,
Wisely, like me, his blows rebuff;
    And never let us part, old friend.

That birthday flown, when first I wore you,
    I mind well—memory yet is strong—
My friends around to honour bore you,
    And poured their welcome forth in song.
Your shabby plight—of which I'm vain—
    Hinders them not an arm to lend,
They'd freely feast us now again;
    So never let us part, old friend.

TO AN OLD COAT.

You're patched behind, an ancient rending;
   That, too, recalls a past delight:
One night to run from Jane pretending,
   I felt her soft hand clutch me tight.
Torn were you, and that frightful tear
   It took my Jane two days to mend,
Whilst I was held her captive there;
   So never let us part, old friend.

Have you been steeped in musk and amber,
   Which fops sniff, looking in the glass?
Or pushed along an ante-chamber,
   For swells to sneer at as we pass?
Throughout all France by faction rent,
   Ribbons and stars fell strife can send—
A field-flower is *your* ornament;
   So never let us part, old friend.

Fear no more days of idle ranging,
   When our two fates became as one,
Of pleasure with pain interchanging,
   Of intermingled rain and sun.
For the last time I soon shall doff
   My clothes, just wait! and we will wend
Together, gently going off;
   So never let us part, old friend.

THE HORSE OF THE DESERT.

(FOUNDED ON AN ARABIC POEM, GIVEN IN GENERAL DAUMAS'S
"CHEVAUX DU SAHARA.")

My steed is black—my steed is black,
    As a moonless and starless night;
He was foaled in wide deserts without a track,
    He drinks the wind in fight;
So drank the wind his sire before him,
And high of blood the dam that bore him.
    In days when the hot war-smoke rises high
My comrades hail him as the unwinged flier,
His speed outstrips the very lightning fire;—
    May God preserve him from each evil eye.

Like the gazelle's his ever-quivering ears,
His eyes gleam softly as a woman's, when
    Her looks of love are full;
His nostrils gape, dark as the lion's den,
And, in the shock of battle, he uprears
    The forehead of a bull.
His flanks, his neck, his shoulders, all are long,

THE HORSE OF THE DESERT.

His legs are flat, his quarters clean and round,
Snake-like his tail shoots out, his hocks are strong,
Such as the desert ostrich bear along,
And his lithe fetlocks spurn the echoing ground.
    As my own soul I trust him, without fear,
    No mortal ever yet bestrode his peer.

His flesh is as the zebra's firm, he glides
    Fox-like, whilst cantering slow across the plain;
    But, when at speed, his limbs put on amain
The wolf's long gallop, and untiring strides.
Yes, in one day he does the work of five;
    No spur his spirit wakes,
But each strung vein and sinew seems alive
    At every bound he makes.
Over the pathless sand, he darteth, straight
As God's keen arrow from the bow of fate;
Or like some thirsty dove, first of the flock,
Towards water hidden in a hollow rock.
A war-horse true, when sinks the clash of swords,
    He loves to hound the lion to his lair;
Glory, with booty won from alien hordes,
    And the soft voices of our virgins fair,
        Fill him with fierce delight.
When on his back through peril's heart I break,
His neighings call the vultures down, and shake
    Each foeman's soul with sudden fright;
On him I fear not Death, she shrinks aside,
Scared by the echoing thunder of his stride.

My darling says, "Come, come to me alone,
"Through night and silence come to me, mine own."
  (O stranger, from beyond the howling seas,
    Leave, leave those flowers,
    Whose bloom is ours,
  To the love-murmur of their native bees.)
Then, by some sweet and subtle instinct taught,
He learns to read aright each secret thought.
  Obedient to the impulse which I feel,
  As to my hand this lifeless steel,
Like a hawk, sweeping homeward to her nest,
    Strong in his quenchless will,
    He rushes onward still,
That I may clasp the loved-one to my breast;
  But whilst I lay me down, with happy sighs,
  Under the light of those entrancing eyes;
In some secluded spot, beyond her door,
  With countless dangers near, he stands alone,
  As if his fiery heart were changed to stone;
And champs his bit till I return once more.
By our great Prophet's head, this matchless horse
  Is the true pearl of every caravan;
The light and life of all our camps,—the force
    And glory of his clan.

  Born, when the war-shout wakes, to lead,
    I am an Arab scheich,
  My flocks are there the poor to feed,
    My name guards well the weak.

The stranger from my father's tent
  Is never turned aside,
For God His choicest gifts hath lent,
  And blessed me far and wide;
But if change come, and angry Fate
  Hold forth her bitter cup to drink,
The path of honour still is straight,
  From thence I shall not shrink.
I shall live nobly yet, if ills are borne
    In patient trust;
I shall be rich enough, if I can scorn
    The sordid lust
Of gold, and look for happier days, to bloom
Beyond the night-frost of the tomb.
  Yea, though Misfortune's iron hand
    Should smite me with her heaviest rod,
  I shall be strong enough to stand
    And praise the name of God.

THE MAMELUKE CHARGE.

LET the Arab courser go
Headlong on the silent foe;
Their plumes may shine like mountain snow,
Like fire their iron tubes may glow,
Their cannon death on death may throw,
Their pomp, their pride, their strength, we know,
But—let the Arab courser go.

   The Arab horse is free and bold,
His blood is noble from of old,
Through dams, and sires, many a one,
Up to the steed of Solomon.
He needs no spur to rouse his ire,
His limbs of beauty never tire,
Then, give the Arab horse the rein,
And their dark squares will close in vain.
Though loud the death-shot peal, and louder,
He will only neigh the prouder;
Though nigh the death-flash glare, and nigher,
He will face the storm of fire;

He will leap the mound of slain,
Only let him have the rein.
The Arab horse will not shrink back,
Though death confront him in his track
The Arab horse will not shrink back,
And shall his rider's arm be slack?
No!—By the God who gave us life,
Our souls are ready for the strife.
We need no serried lines, to show
A gallant bearing to the foe.
We need no trumpet to awake
The thirst, which blood alone can slake.
What is it that can stop our course,
Free riders of the Arab horse?
Go—brave the desert wind of fire;
Go—beard the lightning's look of ire;
Drive back the ravening flames, which leap
In thunder from the mountain steep;
But dream not, men of fifes and drums,
To stop the Arab when he comes:
Not tides of fire, not walls of rock,
Could shield you from that earthquake shock.
Come, brethren, come, too long we stay,
The shades of night have rolled away,
Too fast the golden moments fleet,
Charge, ere another pulse has beat;
Charge—like the tiger on the fawn,
Before another breath is drawn.

LINES ON THE SALE OF THE BLACK ARAB.

THE GIFT OF THE IMÁUM OF MUSCAT TO WILLIAM THE FOURTH:
SOLD BY AUCTION SHORTLY AFTER HIS DEATH.

YES! it is well that he should go,
    The matchless present of a king,
From ends so vile, and thoughts so low,
    As round the soul of England cling.

He was a horse for days of old,
    When British hearts were firm and true,
Unfit for times so mean and cold,
    And *that* the greedy pedlars knew;

They cared not, when to stranger-men
    The courteous monarch's gift was sent;
That linked therewith, for ever then
    The honour of the people went.

They care not that the shameful tale
    Throughout the wavering East is borne,
Making the sellers, and the sale,
    A mark for just and hostile scorn.

What though with throbbing hearts we fear
    Strange terrors rushing from afar,
And daily rather feel than hear
    The stealthy tread of Russian war?

Great thoughts, great deeds, and feelings high,
    The sunshine of our British past,
All they can neither sell nor buy,
    To heaven or hell away they cast.

Yes! it is well that he should go,
    The matchless present of a king,
From ends so vile, and thoughts so low,
    As round the soul of England cling.

The spirit of his Arab sires
    Would droop, as though in fetters bound,
With no reflection of its fires,
    From aught that moved or breathed around.

England of yore was full of men,
    Made strong to run a glorious course,
Of lion-port and eagle-ken,
    Fit riders for the Arab horse.

His high heart, then, like mingling flame,
    Into their brightness would have flowed:
And, in his generous veins, the same
    Free spirit would have lived and glowed.

Such were the fearless few who stood
    Around a trembling tyrant's throne,
Eager to shed their dearest blood
    On Freedom's primal altar-stone.

Such were the giants who upsprung
    Round her who crushed insulting Spain,
When, from our arms and hearts, we flung
    The fragments of the papal chain.

Such who, in old manorial halls,
    Which yet with loyal echoes ring,
Live still along the storied walls
    In armour for an outraged king:

Knights who at Naseby stood, and died
    Unbroken by the Roundhead boor,
Or from broad breast-wounds swelled the tide
    Of faithful blood on Marston Moor.

But Faith, and Truth, and Chivalry,
    And emanating powers, have fled;
The veins of the worn earth are dry,
    By which each mighty growth was fed.

Scarce, through the gathering dimness, One
    True-hearted heir of ancient worth,
Shines, like the last ray of the sun,
    The night before the floods went forth.

The rest are shadows of an hour,
   A sapless, bloodless, boneless throng,
Without the spirit, or the power,
   For noble right, or strenuous wrong.

Amid the fog, and icy gloom,
   Round withered heart, and stunted brain,
We have not sympathy, or room
   For aught that shows a generous strain.

Then freely let the Arab go,
   That matchless present of a king,
From ends so vile, and thoughts so low,
   As round the soul of England cling.

LINES ON A WHITE CYCLAMEN BROUGHT FROM JERUSALEM.

Young blossom! delicately pure and fair,
   Ere sunshine's touch hath warmed the snow-chilled sod;
How comest thou to this grim Northern air,
                  Flower from the land of God?

Not to our clime, oh, petals pale and sweet,
   Are ye akin,—our realms of strife and pain,—
Nor born to be down-trodden under feet
                  Still hurrying after gain;

Thy home is on each holy mountain-side,
   O'er plains filled with the wind-flower's flaming gleam,
O'er dells where the massed oleanders hide,
                  In rose-clouds the blue stream.

Thou bringest back those deathless moments when
   Thy native heaven grew strong with solemn powers,
And breathest here—A type of other men,
                  And other lives, than ours.

LINES ON A WHITE CYCLAMEN.

Yes! above all, thy leaflets fresh and white,
   White as the unreached snows that never wane,
Recall the Man who walked thy hills in light,
               That spirit without stain.

For, whilst thy virgin grace above may show
   How spotless His clear life, the tinge of red
Beneath that purity is whispering low
               Of Blood for sinners shed.

So that, whene'er within us is renewed
   The thought how worn by long unsleeping hours,
He moved across thy Syrian solitude,
               Through a wild wealth of flowers;

We feel that He, sustained by love alone,
   Was there to commune with white stars, and greet
More than all growths by spring around Him thrown,
               Thy white pearls at His feet.

And hence we dream, if dreams may thus presume,
   No fire-flash poured from the anemone,
No oleander's hot and eager bloom,
               Spoke to His heart like thee.

Bring then to winters withering up with cold,
   A balm lent from thy south—To souls that pine
Here hunger-bitten with the lust of gold,
               Memories and hopes divine.

RIZPAH, DAUGHTER OF AIAH.

(WRITTEN FOR MUSIC.)

I.

UNDER the changing sky,
   Under the clouded moon,
The earth gapes, white and dry,
   But the rain cometh soon;
Yes! down from yon low skies
   Rushes, at length, the rain;
Woman forlorn, arise!
   Thou hast not crouched in vain,
       Rizpah, daughter of Aiah.

II.

Brave men have told the king,
   How, scared away by thee,
Each ravenous fowl takes wing,
   And wolves and panthers flee:
How thou hast wrestled here,
   Despising ease and sleep,
Without a thought of fear,
   Because thy love is deep,
       Rizpah, daughter of Aiah.

III.

Therefore, in sight of all,
   A proud tomb is begun,
To hold the bones of Saul,
   And Jonathan, his son;
There too, in calm repose,
   From insult safe, shall dwell
The stately forms of those
   Whom thou hast watched so well,
      Rizpah, daughter of Aiah.

IV.

And whilst the ages roll
   Through time's unsounded deep,
Thy true and tender soul
   A magic life shall keep;
Maidens shall muse alone,
   And mothers' hearts be stirred,
Where'er thy deeds are known,
   Where'er thy name is heard,
      Rizpah, daughter of Aiah.

THE DUKE'S FUNERAL.

1852.

CHILD, with fresh cheek upon thy velvet palm,
O bright-haired child, That sleep is sweet and calm—
Through all those youthful pulses breathing balm;
    But yet I say, Arise!
  The unexhausted night hangs damp—
  Black yet round each unwaning lamp;
  Against the echoing casement-pane,
  Driving raw cold and plangent rain,
    The wind of Autumn sighs.
  Yet from that flowerlike rest, through all,
  Rough gales that blow, chill showers that fall,
    I say again, Arise!
  This once let sleep depart, for lo!
  The hour that seals a nation's woe
  Moves, like a mourner, sad and slow
    Behind yon eastern skies.
The sword of God has fallen unsparing,
  A life is done, a goal is won,
  The sands of a glorious race are run,

And a great people grieveth, bearing
  Home to his grave their noblest son.
  I rouse thee not, because a sight,
    A proud and pompous show,
  Such as enchants the young, ere night
    Through crowded streets will go:
No; but in thee a beacon-light must glow,
A stream of reverence rise to life and flow;
Through thee, from booming gun and muffled drum,
A voice must pass to all the years that come!
  It is to thee, and such as thee,
    That England, great as yet, and free,
      Commits a solemn trust;
  To print, as in a living book,
  On youth's keen brain, each word, each look,
  And mark how o'er the nation's friend,
  By all poor honours earth can lend,
  Our stricken country seeks relief
  From passionate and noble grief.
  So may ye nevermore forget
  In souls unborn a seed to set,
  And kindle hearts unmoulded yet,
    When we are laid in dust.
  That Times and Realms afar may scan
  What England honoured in a man—
  May keep, wherever Freedom's speech,
  And Freedom's island blood, shall reach,
    Though cycles lie between, and oceans sever—
    The Duke's great name a household word for ever.

THE DUKE'S FUNERAL.

See how the people gathereth together,
　　All thoughts of self disdaining !—
How feeble women, in the stormy weather,
　　Stand worn, but uncomplaining !
Rejoicing, rather, thus to show
Their deep sense of the debt they owe.

Why is that people banded thus together,
　　Under the whirling showers?
Why silently endure the sullen weather
　　Throughout these sunless hours?
It is because they here await
The coming of the good and great ;
The man who, down to death, from youth,
Steered by the living star of truth ;
Made his loved country's cause his own,
And saved her for herself alone.
Therefore the Queen upon her throne
　　Weeps bitter tears to-day ;
Therefore the humblest workman here
Bares a rough head before the bier,
When that which was the Duke draws near.
Therefore the soldiers sadly, proudly,
　　Move on their mournful way ;
Therefore the cannon boometh loudly
　　Athwart the fog-smoke gray ;
Therefore the leaders of the State
Around the gorgeous pageant wait,
And chiefs from many a land afar,

From proud and distant kings,
Each wise in peace or brave in war,
   His sign of reverence brings.

The car through silence groaneth on,
   Beneath a hero's earthly part;
Blind nerves and brain, whose work is done—
   True servants to the flawless heart
     Of England's worthiest son.
Yes! and before the world we say
That it is right in open day
(Though to the worm's surrendered prey)
These rites and honours thus to pay;
Since this for that frail form we claim,
That never, since the birth of fame,
     Did mortal frame
     Of any name
Inscribed on Glory's dazzling roll,
Swerve less from Duty's calm control,
Or send to God a nobler soul.
So let the martial music flow around,
   The soldiers mourn their chief;
And muffled drums, with melancholy sound,
   Fill all the air with grief.

It is an hour when bright hopes darken,
   When strong hearts fail through fear,
As for the coming storm they hearken,
   With him no longer here.

With gathering clouds of omen spread,
The hot sky gloometh overhead;
The fevered earth, the restless deep,
Are trembling, as in troubled sleep,
And on the nations, like a pall,
Black shadows from the future fall.
Vague terrors haunt our failing hearts,
But he, by God's high grace, departs,
And, ere the mighty tempest breaks,
To other, nobler life awakes,
From his long toil by Heaven set free,
Whilst yet there seemed tranquillity.
So, on his throne of airy gold,
Serenely sank that sun of old
The night before the waves were rolled
In raging masses uncontrolled;
When earth's great deep, by angels rent asunder,
Upheaved its sable fountain-floods in thunder,
From fathomless abysses still renewing
Sea after sea to overwhelm and ruin.

But let the Future, for one hour,
    In God's almighty hand repose;
Let no forebodings dim have power
    To mar the glorious close
Of that great life, whose iron will
Said to advancing Fate, Be still!
The shattered universe re-cast,
And staunched the death-wound of the past.

THE DUKE'S FUNERAL.

The Past, the Past, with him and glory fraught,
To-day is lord of ear, and eye, and thought.

    Who knows not how that orb sublime
        Its matchless course has run?
    It were an idle waste of time
        To show the noon-day sun.
    Enough, that when the ruthless Gaul
        Became on earth the scourge of God,
    When one man moved the Lord of All,
        And crushed a people where he trod—
    His dauntless heart in stedfast ardour burned
        With that gigantic foe to cope,
    His eagle eye on distant hills discerned
        The sunrise of a living hope.[1]
    Thence undismayed, through lands afar,
    With steady motion like a star
    That knows not haste, nor doubt, nor rest,
    Still on, and on, and on he pressed:
    Till from that Titan, prostrate and forlorn,
        That soul of iron mixed with clay,
    The purple mantle of his pride was torn,
        The strong sword wrenched away.

Then first our hero paused (whilst Europe shed
Her stars, and crowns, like snow-flakes round his head),
And though he sought not glory, found his name
The light that filled the golden skies of fame.

        [1] Torres Vedras.

What paths in after-years he trod,
　　And how he played his part;
Is it not written by the hand of God
　　Upon the people's heart?
All now is over, we have looked our last,
　　His light is quenched, his tale is told;
He joins at length, in glory unsurpassed,
　　The mighty men of old.
So let the martial music flow around,
　　The soldiers mourn their chief;
And muffled drums, with melancholy sound,
　　Fill all the air with grief.

Child, suns must rise and set, the earth
　　Through years and cycles onward roam;
And ever, past the gates of Death and Birth,
　　Life's ocean-tide exhaustless foam.
We soon must leave thee—soon wilt thou be sitting
　　Serenely under silver hair;
Whilst bright curls glance, and fairy forms are flitting
　　Around thy venerable chair.
Then wilt thou tell them, "Years and years ago,
　　"(I took it as a thing of course),
" An old man used to pass me, stooping low,
　　" White-headed, on his horse.

　" I took it as a thing of course
" Till that pale rider, often watched unknown,
" To the soul's insight, through the eye, was shown.

"A voice proclaimed, 'That drooping form, of yore,
"'Through seas of blood upheld, through earthquakes bore
"'His country safe to Peace's golden shore.
"'That feeble hand, which scarce can grasp the reins,
"'Like God's own thunder shivered Europe's chains.
"'Mark well the reverent head, the locks of snow,
  "'They will not long be here;
"''Tis more for thee than thou canst feel or know,
  "'To see the Duke so near.'"
Then will those children, round the fire at night,
Keep ever asking of this mournful sight,
Drinking, with ever new delight,
The tale of each heroic fight,
When England conquered in the right;
Then, whilst young eyes gleam fiercely bright,
 Young faces flush, as if with wine,
Remember *why* we led thee forth ere light,
 And let such words as these be thine:—

"His deeds in war were great, but greater still
"That high clear spirit, that unfaltering will!
"His intellect all honoured, not so much
"For gifts which dazzle wheresoe'er they touch,
"As that in him calm courage, zeal like fire,
"Which, when fate darkened, only blazed the higher,
"And patient justice, that no wrongs could tire,
"Enriched a simple soul without pretence,
"And to rare genius raised its common sense.
"He was by all beloved, but less because

"His sword had triumphed in his country's cause,
    "Than that men knew
    "His life was true,
"That, when he saw his duty, power and pelf,
"All lust of glory, and all thoughts of self,
    "Away like dross he threw;
"That, nor ambition's lures, nor wounded pride,
  "Nor malice of unjust rebuke,
"From honour's instant path could turn aside
  "One foot-mark of the Iron Duke."

    This is what thou hast to say
    To to-morrow from to-day;
    This is why the land wept o'er him,
    And as one man the people bore him
    To sleep where Nelson slept before him.

Alas! in vain all rosy from his cot
  The child of hope was roused upon that morn,
He died, when England called him, pausing not;
  And left us here with broken hearts forlorn.

                      Oct. 1883.

NAPOLEON THE IDOL.

(FROM THE FRENCH OF BARBIER.)

Quick, Foreman, quick, wood-coal and pit-coal throw,
    Tin, copper, iron, toss them there—
With huge arm fiercely raking to and fro,
    Like an old Vulcan, feed the flare.

A mighty meal to the vast furnace bring,
    For if those teeth are meant to bite,
And chew the ores you to his gullet fling,
    That palate roof must flame with light.

'Tis well—the mad fires burst in wrath at large,
    Blood-red and pitiless they wake:
Whilst rolling down they sound their battle charge,
    Out-flanked and clubbed the metals break—

With one delirious bound and yell and throe
    Copper on tin, on iron rolls
Tin fused, all twists, all twines, as far below
    In Hell deep-vaulted three damned souls.

NAPOLEON THE IDOL.

At length the work is done—the lights have died,
    The white heat fades to ashen gray—
Whilst yet the mass boils hard, fling, Foreman, wide
    Thy gates, and give the tide its way.

Oh! rushing river sweep along thy bed,
    With one dart forth, one impulse pour
Thyself, as cataracts flash from over-head,
    As flames from a volcano roar.

The earth's breast gapes to clasp your lava wave,
    Dash down, one raging mass, amain,
Into that mould of steel, dash down a slave,
    And straight an emperor rise again.

Napoleon yet—once more that Titan's frame ;
    Ah! what a price he made us pay,
The soldier grim, in blood and tears and shame,
    For certain paltry sprigs of bay.

Sad—sad for France—the tortured and down-flung,
    When tottering on its lofty base,
Like some poor thief, his earlier statue hung
    On cruel cords in empty space.

And, when by ceaseless efforts overthrown,
    Head-first that proud and king-like mass
Tumbled at speed, then on the frozen stone
    Rolled, rattling down its corpse of brass,

The Hun of skin that stinks, the stupid Hun,
    His eyes with drunken anger red,
Before all France, where filthiest gutters run,
    Dragged through the dirt our Emperor's head.

On all who keep a heart their breasts within,
    Weighs like a sense of guilt that day,
It is a brand on each French brow, burnt in,
    Which nought but Death can cleanse away.

I saw beneath our marbles shadowing,
    The invader crowd his heavy wains,
And strip our trees, as food their bark to fling,
    For horses from his Scythian plains.

I saw the Northman stern of aspect beat
    Our blackened flesh, and never spare,
Till the blood sprung; they came our bread to eat,
    And fill their foul lungs with our air.

Well, through those days of pain, of evil fate,
    Of nameless horrors undergone,
There was but one on whom I flung my hate,
    Accursed be thou—Napoleon.

Oh, straight-haired Corsican, was not France fair
    'Neath those grand suns of Messidor?
A dauntless and untameable blood-mare,
    Nor steel bit, nor gold reins she wore.

A courser wild, her rough flanks all a-glow
  With gore from kings that reeked, plunged she;
Her proud feet sharply smote the earth below,
  Our earth then, for the first time, free.

No hand had yet bent down that stately crest,
  To stain her beauty, or disturb,
On her broad loins no saddle had been prest,
  Nor knew she yet a stranger's curb.

Her bright coat gleamed, as wandering like the wind,
  With keen eye, and limbs never still,
Poised on firm hocks, she terrified mankind,
  With her defiant neighings shrill.

You came and saw her beautiful and young,
  With quarters rippling as she stept,
Grasping her mane, a Centaur bold and strong,
  High-booted on her back you leapt.

Then as she loved the sound of war, the force
  Of powder, and the drum's fierce roll,
All earth you gave her for her Beacon-course,
  And battles to delight her soul.

Then no more peace, no hope from sleep or night
  Still new skies, motion and unrest,
She crushed like sand men's bodies in her flight,
  With blood-gouts splashing round her breast.

Thus fifteen years her hard foot smiting fast,
    Hurled generations to the ground,
Thus fifteen years at reeking speed she past
    O'er prostrate millions strewed around.

Till wearied of her ceaseless gallop there,
    Of roads to a goal never brought,
Of trampling worlds, and scattering on the air
    Like dust, the lives of men for nought,

With spent breath tottering by in weak despair,
    At every stride about to fall,
She prayed the Corsican who rode, to spare—
    You, cut-throat, listened not at all.

Hard and more hard your sinewy thighs pressed home,
    To quench the low moans from beneath,
You wrenched the curb about her mouth all foam,
    And broke in reckless wrath her teeth.

She rose once more for her last battle-plain,
    But with no strength the bit to hold,
Then on a bed of grape she dropped again,
    And crushed you as in death she rolled.

From that dread fall, as by a second birth,
    Like the bright eagle rising high,
You mount again to lord it over earth,
    And float re-plumed along the sky.

NAPOLEON THE IDOL.

No more that thief of crowns—Napoleon,
   That brigand, shameless, false, and coarse,
Who pressed the choking cushions of his throne
   On Freedom's throat, without remorse.

No more that galley-slave who died despairing
   On his black rock, and dragged his heel,
The thought of France like felon's bullet wearing
   Beneath the stranger's scourge of steel.

Not so—no stain upon the Emperor stays,
   Thanks to each flatterer's utterance, thanks
To lying poets belching forth his praise,
   'Mid Cæsar gods, a god he ranks.

His presence lights each wall once more,
   His name in every public street
Sounds, as of old through the grim battle's roar
   It sounded from the drums that beat.

Whilst from each height, where swarms the populace,
   Drops Paris, like a pilgrim old,
And day by day, at the tall column's base,
   Bows in the dust her forehead bold.

There grasping loads of bay, born but to die,
   And tossing flower-floods ever new
To that bronze, where can rest no mother's eye,
   Since under mothers' tears it grew,

To fife and clarion, drunk with maniac glee,
    Around the great Napoleon—France
Keeps up, though drest in work-day garb she be,
    The riot of her reckless dance.

Move on then—oh, tame shepherds of mankind,
    Kings of meek spirit—go your way!
Wise—but with foreheads of that vulgar kind,
    Which throws not back Fame's dazzling ray.

By you men's fetters are struck off in vain,
    In vain, because you lead and save,
Your flocks unvext without or toil or pain,
    Reach their long rest within the grave.

Soon as your guiding stars have ceased to be,
    Whilst their last light dies down apace,
Each failing name, along Time's boundless sea,
    Scarce marks its momentary trace.

Move on—move on—for you no statues rise,
    Your work the Future knoweth not,
The only Lord of living memories,
    Is he who kills with sword, or shot.

Man worships him, by whom moist fields are hid
    Beneath a heap of putrid bones,
He loves the builder of the pyramid,
    Who breaks each back to move his stones.

The people is a tap-room wench, who likes
　　To quaff the harsh new wine, and yearns
To find a lover with a fist that strikes,
　　An iron frame, an eye that burns.

She, couched on straw in her foul garret's height,
　　Can love none but the Rough, whose way
Is to beat hard, and maul her all the night—
　　The livelong night—till dawns the day.

THE EPICUREAN.

How gently, beautiful and calm,
   The quiet river murmurs by;
How soft the light, how full of balm
   The breeze that soothes the dark'ning sky!

In every clime, in every state,
   We may be happy if we will;
Man wrestles against iron fate,
   And then complains of pain and ill.

The flowers, the beasts, the very heaven,
   Calmly their destined paths pursue;
All take the pleasures that are given,
   We only find them short and few.

Oh that mankind, alive to truth,
   Would cease a hopeless war to wage;
Would reap in youth, the joys of youth,—
   In age, the peacefulness of age!

Upon an everlasting tide
  Into the silent seas we go;
But verdure laughs along the side,
  And roses on the margin blow.

Nor life, nor death, nor aught they hold,
  Rate thou above their natural height;
Yet learn that all our eyes behold,
  Has value, if we mete it right.

Pluck then the flowers that line the stream,
  Instead of fighting with its power;
But pluck as flowers, not gems, nor deem
  That they will bloom beyond their hour.

Whate'er betides, from day to day,
  An even pulse and spirit keep;
And like a child, worn out with play,
  When wearied with existence, sleep.

THE PLATONIST.

Father of Gods and men, on thee we call,
   Thou, who within the limits of thy soul,
Embracing all things, yet distinct from all,
   Spread'st life and order through the boundless whole.

It is the highest privilege of man,
   The crown, which philosophic virtue brings,
After long years of thought, aright to scan
   Thy presence, hidden under human things.

Not easy is the task—nor is it wise,
   At large the holy secret to unfold;
Excessive light, into dim-seeing eyes,
   Infuses darkness blinder than of old.

How noble are the Gods—that spring from thee,
   The holy ones who made and bless us all—
Rivers of goodness, issuing from thy sea
   Of love, into whose deeps again they fall.

And we too are thy children, for within
    Our dim and crowded hearts, under the strife
Of fleshly lusts, of passion, and of sin,
    Burns on one spark of everlasting life.

A spark of heaven is given us, to keep clear
    Of this foul dungeon's damp, that we may see,
A seed of heaven is set, for us to rear,
    Into a beautiful and deathless tree.

For this the toilsome circle was ordained,
    Lives new and multiform, unending still—
Until the soul its native seats has gained,
    Or sunk for ever to the gulfs of ill.

Turn not the spirit into flesh, nor grieve
    For virtue's sake to suffer and to die—
So, after fewer transits, shalt thou leave
    Gross darkness, for a shining light on high.

THE FUSILIERS' DOG.

LATELY RUN OVER AFTER HAVING GONE THROUGH THE CRIMEAN CAMPAIGN.

Go lift him gently from the wheels,
    And soothe his dying pain,
For love and care e'en yet he feels,
    Though love and care be vain;
'Tis sad that, after all these years,
    Our comrade and our friend,
The brave dog of the Fusiliers,
    Should meet with such an end.

Up Alma's hill, among the vines,
    We laughed to see him trot,
Then frisk along the silent lines,
    To chase the rolling shot:
And, when the work waxed hard by day,
    And hard and cold by night;
When that November morning lay
    Upon us, like a blight,

And eyes were strained, and ears were bent,
   Against the muttering north,
Till the gray mist took shape, and sent
   Gray scores of Russians forth—
Beneath that slaughter wild and grim,
   Nor man nor dog would run;
He stood by us, and we by him,
   Till the great fight was done.

And right throughout the snow and frost
   He faced both shot and shell;
Though unrelieved, he kept his post,
   And did his duty well.
By death on death the time was stained,
   By want, disease, despair;
Like autumn leaves our army waned,
   But still the dog was there:

He cheered us through those hours of gloom;
   We fed him in our dearth;
Through him the trench's living tomb,
   Rang loud with reckless mirth;
And thus, when peace returned once more,
   After the city's fall,
That veteran home in pride we bore,
   And loved him, one and all.

With ranks re-filled, our hearts were sick,
   And to old memories clung;

The grim ravines we left glared thick
   With death-stones of the young.
Hands which had patted him lay chill,
   Voices which called were dumb,
And footsteps that he watched for still
   Never again could come.

Never again; this world of woe
   Still hurries on so fast;
They come not back, 'tis he must go
   To join them in the past:
There, with brave names and deeds entwined,
   Which time may not forget,
Young Fusiliers unborn shall find
   The legend of our pet.

Whilst o'er fresh years, and other life
   Yet in God's mystic urn,
The picture of the mighty strife
   Arises sad and stern—
Blood all in front, behind far shrines
   With women weeping low,
For whom each lost one's fame but shines,
   As shines the moon on snow.

THE SIRENS.

All the old tales of evil beauty in the Grecian mythology are, I think, tales of the sea, probably therefore of Phœnician origin; at any rate, the idea of evil beauty is not in accordance with the general character of the Greek mind. I have endeavoured to obviate this anomaly, by making the Sirens the unwilling instruments of a destiny which they can neither explain nor resist.

No rest—no pause—no change—Achnymene,
And thou, Phenusa, with thy shadowing hair
Thrown round the weepings of a heart outworn
To veil them from the sight—Belovèd ones,
Speak to me: is there any hope for us
But in ourselves? have we not inward strength
And sinews of the spirit, to control
This self-surrender to the powers of ill?

What though, like hovering clouds, about our home,
Slow moving ever to the moving sea,
Drift undulating ships—there—moss-grown rafts,
The spoil of Caucasus, compact with oak,
And rough primeval pine-trees interlaced;
Floating of old beneath gigantic forms

Who, urged by power malign, were hurried on
Down forest-shadowed rivers sounding wide,
To the great deep; thence under hostile stars
With rude art skirting this accursèd shore.
Here—tall Sidonian barks—Ægean boats
Built low for speed; and of the jealous isle
Full freighted argosies, for whose return
Even now the merchant kings are looking out
From the broad quays of Tyre—magnificent
With gold and pearl, and tribute from afar.

What though the breath of our entrancing song
Heaps up, from age to age, around our feet
The mouldering bones of men, as the keen gales
Over Numidia wide accumulate
Incessant hills of ever-heightening sand:
Still, oh, belovèd sisters, not by us
Is the life drawn away out of the heart;
Not upon us, relentless Destinies,
The curse of the bereavèd rests—hour after hour,
Day after day, year after year, for ever,
Our prayers have wearied the vast halls of heaven
That we might spare—but the Fates, iron-nerved,
Press close upon us, irremoveably,
And we but struggle, like a dragon writhing
Its hopeless folds under a steadfast rock.

Still, as the white sail from the distant sea
Uprises, slowly thickening into form

Above its peopled hull, our better nature
Glides from us like the shadow of a dream:
Still, the unbodied demons with fierce glee,
And ravenous exactness, streaming up
From some unsounded depth of Acheron,
Pass into us, and shake the vacant soul
With phantoms swarming from an evil will.
So that, instead of feeling gentle thoughts
And impulses of love, and happy hopes
Blossoming, one by one, like summer flowers,
As, in the days of old, when cherishing
A life, serenely passionless, yet soft,
We fed on beauty, beauty in all forms,
In all her aspects, ministrant on good.
Now fettered to some demon lord unknown,
And doomed to execute his purposes,
We rush through horrible vicissitudes
Of stormy sin—passion—and pain—and change—
We shudder in an unimagined thirst
For human blood, in fits of hideous crime,
Alien desires, undreamt-of attributes,
And all the heat and darkness of deep hell—
Full thence of awful fever, we become
A chaos of commingling elements
Working within, and smothering as they spread
The sense of beauty, and the touch of good,
Till the foul mist dissolving, rushes out
In floods of sound, and headlong melodies,
Enriching the insatiate nets of death:

Whilst, ever pressing in upon the brain,
The air of heaven grows heated like a sea
Of fluctuating fires around, through which
Pale features and faint shapes are dimly seen,
Immoveably decaying, with bright eyes,
And indrawn breathings of hushed ecstacy.
Until, the purpose being accomplished,
Back to his home the demon speeds, and we,
Wildered and weak and panting, find ourselves
Among the silent faces of the dead, upon
The broadly blossoming shores of the full sea.
Say, what avails it then, when we behold
The breathless aspect of the beautiful
Waning from beauty, or the loving heart
Shining unquenchable through dying eyes—
Say, what avails it, that we crowd the night
With moaning upon moaning, and repel
All thoughts of pleasure, and all hope of rest?
Girt, if we sleep, with ghastly multitudes,
Which wax and wane, and sever and combine,
And flit, and glare, and fade; as others still
Keep flickering up from the dim gulf of dreams,
To die past deaths again—Gaunt mariners,
And bright-haired women, and the steel-clad strength
Of old sea-kings, with garments rich and strange,
And visages burnt in upon the brain—
So that our worn hearts, empty of delight,
Are wasted utterly, and drop away
In bitter weepings.—I have wept enough—

THE SIRENS.

Year after year, in vague self-torturings,
I have stood nightly on moon-lighted cliffs
Near the soft-sounding ocean—I have called
The everlasting stars to answer me
From their bright quietness; I have invoked
Forgotten names and forms of ancient gods—
Ophion, and the mystic three who droop
From fading thrones, among the caverns old,
And on the clouded hills of Samothrace.
But not from these, nor from the younger heavens
Filled with rejoicing gods, nor from beneath,
When, maddened with the sickness of suspense,
I have thrown loathing off, and called aloud
To the swart powers of sullen Erebus,
Down deepening through his separate gulfs of death.—
Nor yet from that far God—the nameless one—
The everlasting, the unsearchable—
Who in his fathomless infinitude
Clasps equally the undivulged abyss
Of darkness and the inmost home of light,—
Has come or voice or token, to unfold
How we, of our own natures full of love,
As are the heavens of day, or the broad sea
Of waters,—in this solitary spot—
This desert isle—remote from Gods and men,
Can thus have earned, of the deaf universe,
Our weary and impenetrable doom.

Therefore, uplifting from my soul the load

Of the drear past—let the unanswering stars,
And the void air, and the unpitying heaven
Feel sorrow for the dead—*I* weep no more—
I will no longer yield my spirit up
To this—I will no longer be the slave
Of such forlorn and futile sympathies.
There is yet music sleeping in the lute,
Soft airs, and modulations, over which
There hangeth not the taint of human blood :
There are yet glories of the earth and sea,
And splendours in the sky—nor from the heart
Is absent the deep sense of solemn joy,
Which rushes like a river, loosed from ice,
To greet the coming of the beautiful.
To them—to it—to all—to life and hope,
To poesy and nature, to the light
Of Loveliness, and the calm powers of Joy,
I dedicate myself.   There are yet ships
To moulder here, there are yet men to die—
But what of that ?   Death is the end of all—
There are a thousand paths, a thousand gates
On silent hinges ever opening in
To his black hall, so has it been decreed !
We are no more than one blind instrument,
One of the countless multitude, employed
To lead the shadowy sons of time and change,
From heat and dust, from passion and from sin,
To their dim couches of unending rest.
We too shall die—in that unfathomed gloom

There is a place for us, there is a home,
For our world-wearied hearts, encompassèd
With silence, and undreaming weight of sleep.
For ever, and for ever, we shall lie,
After this fitful wretchedness, in death
Taking our fill of rest, with a half-sense
Of something pleasurable sliding down
Throughout the blind abyss, as overhead
The earth renews itself unceasingly
In fruitage, and bright flowers, and everywhere
From her full breast of undecaying youth,
Life gushes into fountains of delight.

THE OLD AGE OF SOPHOCLES.

Πῶς ἔχεις ὦ Σοφόκλεις πρὸς τἀφροδίσια. κ. τ. λ.
PLATO, DE REP. LIB. I.

LEAF-TINTED through the vines, a ray of green
Is playing from the horizontal sun;
Fast, as they reach yon plane-tree's deepening screen,
The silver waters darken as they run;
And there, an old man of majestic mien,
Sitting, with silver hair and eye serene,
Muses on Time and on Eternity—
On the bold hopes in which his youth begun,
The much accomplished, the more left undone:
Draw near with reverence, for this is he
Who heard the eyeless father's cursings wild
Fall on the hostile twins, who called up thee,
High-souled Electra, and that orphan child
Antigone, as lofty, and more mild:

CONTINUED.

Upon the setting sun he gazed, whose light,
An emblem of himself, before him lay,
Poised in mild beauty on the edge of night,
The dreams that dazzled morning with delight,

The splendours of hot noon, had passed away,
And Repose came before the tomb, a sight
Serenely sacred in its calm decay;
For as life faded, underneath the sway
Of an immortal spirit, evermore
Brighter and keener, like a kindling star
Dilating inwardly, the frantic jar
Of struggling lusts, and passions deemed before
Resistless, now became submiss and still,
No more enchaining the distorted will.

CONTINUED.

And men came round him, eager to drink in
That mild paternal wisdom, full of love,
And peace, and shadowy grandeur from above,
A twilight, just becoming the first ray
Of the freed spirit's everlasting day.
But one there was, whom shame could not reprove,
Nor holy age abash—nor wisdom win
To put aside the thoughts of earth and sin.
"Tell me," he cried, "can woman's quickening eye
"Still thaw thee into transient youth, and move
"Thy frozen blood from its thin apathy;
"Or is the sense of pleasure dead within?"
Thus spoke he, either of a scornful mind,
Or to all moral beauty deaf and blind.

CONTINUED.

As if an eagle, whose unfaltering flight
Sweeps through the halls of sunshine, with a range

Wide as the sky, should plunge into a night
Of freezing clouds, before they reached his sight;
Thus, with a sudden sense of painful change,
As into stormy darkness out of light
The hearers passed—Heaven-taught by hopes sublime,
The poet answered, "Thou art yet enthralled
" In the foul webs of sense, be wise in time:
" The privilege of age is to be called
" Out of life's whitening ashes, to a clime
" And region of calm thought, a glorious realm,
" Where Truth and Freedom reign, divine exchange
" For passions which enslave and overwhelm."

CONCLUDED.

Ay! even then, when health and strength sunk low,
When each temptation to indulge desire
Crumbled away upon life's failing fire,
And Earth, with all her gifts, arose to go;
Happy, if even then the soul might show
Some shadow of her origin divine,
And with fresh hopes, and zeal renewed, aspire
To wrestle with her maimed and wearied foe.
Mean though we be, our state through Christ is higher,
A power flows to us from His awful sign,
Which is both spear and shield, wherewith to face
And conquer, though in baleful powers arrayed,
Those unseen kings, to whom man's hapless race
Homage, of old inevitable, paid.

FROM THE COLISEUM AT ROME TO MY WIFE AT NICE: 1848.

WHERE Ruin, at herself aghast,
    Moans round the undying city's wall,
    Where painted church and marble hall
  Are but the plunderers of the Past,
Who here upholds and spreads his mystic sway;
Till the dim Present drops ashamed away;

I see the stars, more ancient still,
    Burn reckless, through the azure skies,
    They care not what beneath them lies,—
  Proud works of human power and skill,
Or spectral peaks, in southern oceans, crowned
With raging fires, all silent ice around.

They care not, in their awful march,
    That empires pass, like clouds, away;
    No shadow, from our world's decay,
  Can darken yon eternal arch;
And though Earth reeled at Rome's expiring cry,
'Twas Earth alone; they heard it not on high.

Time was, when Tiber seaward rolled
   His yellow ripples, all unknown,
   These towers as yet were slumbering stone
And the Seven Hills a nameless wold;
But still, unchangeably, each natural force
Had kept through cycles its appointed course.

Ere Rome was, they were: in decay
   Rome lies,—they feel no touch of age;
   So that the prophet and the sage
Seem here to mock us, when they say
That man's high soul was framed to live and shine
Stronger than time, and more than stars divine.

The hero does not start, to feel our tread,
   More than the slave—we trample both—
   Oscan, Etruscan, Roman, Goth,
All rank together, as The Dead;
And the heart droops, as if by Rome's huge fall
That scythèd skeleton grew lord of all.

Yes, my heart drooped, till suddenly
   Among these tottering temples hoar,
   And tombs forgotten, to its core
Rushed, like fresh blood, a thought of thee;
Through this, Death's home, it seemed to throb and glow,
And link me with the sleeping souls below.

They too had loved: now Thought and Love
   Once kindled, are not quenched, but give

TO MY WIFE AT NICE.

The veins of earth their warmth, and live
To overlast the heavens above :
Man's work may die, his thought, when once unfurled,
Moves on for ever, with the moving world.

And Love than Thought is mightier still,
    Love, who from this majestic Rome,
    Drags me to thee, in spirit, home :
Each trophied arch, each columned hill,
Fades into dimness, as I feel, from far,
Thy spirit dawn upon me like a star,

And on my heart a picture raise
    Of thy soft eyes, in tender joy,
    Bent downwards, whilst our blue-eyed boy
    Eddies around thy smile, and plays
A fountain of sweet laughter, blithe to see
His orange gleaming on its golden tree.

FROM HEINE.

A PINE-TREE standeth lonely
   On a bleak northern hill,
And sleeps with ice surrounded
   With snow that falleth still.

There is one palm he dreams of,
   Far in the morning land,
Who mourns alone, and silent,
   Mid rocks and burning sand.

STANZAS SUGGESTED BY THE ABOVE.

THEY dream, but dreams are of the night;
   Will not the sun rise by and by?
Or is the hope that thirsts for light
   Only a mocking lie?

A wondrous dawn may wake, and turn
   To floods of life the phantom snows,
Whilst desert sands that drift and burn
   Shall blossom as the rose.

STANZAS SUGGESTED BY THE ABOVE.

The pine and palm may feel that then
    Both cold and heat, and Time and Space,
On polar crag, in tropic glen,
    To other laws give place.

Through them, whilst the young heavens grow rife
    With joy, and airs divinely sweet,
Distance dies off from spirit-life,
    That severed hearts may meet.

Oh leave that thought to float above,
    Each parching leaf, each blighted bough;
It breathes of hope, it breathes of love,
    It worketh on—even now,

In that dark pine's despairing breast,
    To melt the bitter frost of pain;
And on his drooping palm-tree's crest
    Falls like the early rain.

CAIUS MANLIUS CAPITOLINUS.

A BALLAD WRITTEN FOR A BOY.

Ever the cold rains gather fast,—ever the cold rains fall,
The summer is a sullen one, throughout the land of Gaul;
The bearded corn droops mixed with mud, the sheep and oxen pine,
And meagre hang the hail-beat grapes around the blasted vine:
The spirit of the nation straight caught from the skies their gloom,
Saw written on each frowning cloud dim signs of coming doom,
And murmured low, in gathering groups, "Some victim must atone—
"Some virgin heart must spot with gore the broad black altar stone—
"That Hesus, pleased with wounds and death, may smile from heaven again;
"And Taranis pour sunshine down in lieu of wasting rain."
Uprose a priest, with hair and beard as white as driven snow,
"Not for this cause, ye tribes," he cried, "the blood of Gaul must flow,

"In the old years, when dearth or time drained dry the
  people's hoards,
" Our fathers took their armour down, and buckled on
  their swords;
" As falcons strike the silver dove, as wolves at sheep-folds
  run,
" We leapt across the mountains on the children of the
  sun :
" Whilst soft Etruscans sat and dreamt, shaping their gems
  and urns;
" Then all the stately magnates paid rich ransom in their
  turns,
" Then were we sure of meat enough, whatever might
  befall,—
" These were the ancient manners and the good old rules
  of Gaul."
The grim clans clashed their gleaming swords, they shouted
  one and all,
" Long live the ancient manners and the good old rules of
  Gaul !"
Right through that night, like angry bees, men rustle to and
  fro,
Huge hammers ring in armourer's booths, and fires unsleep-
  ing glow;
Till sunrise saw the war-stream pour its tides of flame and
  blood,
Through ice-ribbed Alps loud-roaring like Eridanus in flood,
Where'er that war-stream shakes the earth, where'er those
  tides are poured,

Woe to the arm that shapeth gems, and cannot wield a sword—
Woe to the white-walled cities now, perched high o'er purple bays,
Woe to the merry throngs that bind in sheaves the golden maize.
Pale faces, shuddering forms, must soon, through all their terraced lines,
Glide, like dim ghosts that hate the sun, along the silent vines;
Nor shall the moans of men be dumb, nor shrieks of women cease,
Till kings and priests have kissed the feet of drunken churls for peace,
Till prostrate tribes have piled on high their corn and wine and gold,
And bought such scornful mercy as the greedy Northmen sold.
But, though each stream is foul with gore, the wide air choked with groans,
Though thick the smoke of flaming towns, and loud the crash of thrones,
One city still to kneel and bow her haughty head disdains,
For full of iron is the blood that swells the Roman veins;
Born with no soft Ionian soul, nor of a Lydian line,
Woe to the nations against whom her spears in anger shine:
Undreamt of yet, as mystic Time through Heaven's wide orbit sweeps,
An oak within its acorn hid, her mighty future sleeps;

But still, though young, that giant arm, with sword for ever
bare,
And muscles strung to grasp a world, grows strong unheeded
there.
Like a choked stream, that hero-race chafes angrier day by
day,
As moths desire the blasting light they panted for the fray.
In vain their wisest chiefs, whose hair was helmet-worn and
white,
Said, "Autumn suns will soon be here, and winter frosts at
night;
" Let your hearts grow hot in silence, as the heart of Ætna
waits
" To burst in flame that conquers all through her scorched
mountain gates.
"A day will come, in heaven and earth, when sword to
sword shall fall,
" Gradivus upon Hesus, and the Roman on the Gaul;
" But now their mailèd multitudes are like the boundless
sea,
" And midnight voices of the gods forbid the fight to be."
" Tush! tush!" the striplings answered them, "old eyes
are dimmed by fear ;
" Seven Gauls are not too many for each bold young Roman
spear.
" Our tempered steel shall smite at once their feeble glaives
in twain,
" And force those beaten wolves to slink back through their
Alps again."

At once, through all Rome's echoing gates, the joyous squadrons pour;
Hot life-blood of a widowed state, doomed to flow back no more.
In vain Gradivus they invoke, their stern ancestral god,
Whilst iron lines unbroken sink dead on the trampled sod,
As, inch by inch, the glacier grinds o'er earth-fast pines its way,
The massive onset of the Gauls crashed through their strong array;
Till to her nest, on wounded wings, outworn the eagle flew:
Those Gauls were fierce and numberless, her Romans brave, but few.
Of those who went in triumph forth, a scanty band remains,
But still the proud hard spirit lives in those steel-strengthened veins.
Though baffled hate with hostile fire the vacant town devours,
"This hill," they shout, "and Roman swords and Roman souls, are ours!"
And if beneath the leaden weight and pressure of defeat,
In each young breast, at times less free that iron impulse beat,
The wise old men are there to say, "Be firm, and fear not yet:
"The past is past, but your own hearts the future must beget,
"Rome rests on you to rise once more, or in black ruin bow,—

"'Twere an ill cure for rashness then, to shrink and tremble now."
Meanwhile the Gauls, with angered eyes, beheld the calm sun sink
Behind the line of spears which watched the precipice's brink;
Against the chiefs their muttered ire grew loud and louder still,
"The city's ours: what boots it, if the Romans keep the hill?"
Down went the day, but straight the moon unveiled her crescent light,
And through that blue and stainless heaven the stars shone large and white.
"Not yet, not yet, great Taranis the end of Rome decrees,"
Said fierce King Brennus; "We must wait for darker hours than these."
Eve followed eve, and still the moon unveiled an ampler light,
Still through blue depths until the dawn the stars shone large and white,
And still, in spite of savage looks, of hunger and disease,
Said fierce king Brennus, "We must wait for darker hours than these."
In God's good time, when morning broke,[1] gray glooms about it swung,
And deepened round the struggling sun, which faint and rayless hung,

---

[1] 1st of August 1846.

Now strangled in the thicker mist, now half seen through the thin,
The hot world waiting silent till the great storm should begin.
Then came the lightning's blinding flash, which, like some magic key,
Flung wide the dungeons of the air, and set the tempest free.
Long thunders shook the ink-black sky, again, and yet again,
Blue jaggèd fires hissed frequent through the solid sheets of rain,
The short fierce gusts of raving wind roared in the ruined town,
Crash, through the squalls, came half-burnt tower and shattered temple down.
"To arms!" king Brennus cried, "to arms! unheard unmarked shall fall,
"Whilst heaven and earth together reel, the war-step of the Gaul."
The guards above, worn out by toil, and watching long in vain,
Slept on their arms, in spite of all the thunder and the rain;
The sentinels themselves were deaf, each slumbering on his post,
So many nights had passed in peace, nor brought the Gallic host.
Still on that craggy ledge of rock one Roman lay awake,
He heard the cataracts of hail, he heard the thunders break.

He looked to see, at every blaze, in bursts of sudden white,
The marble columns of Jove's fane leap out upon the
    night;
Whilst not less sudden, or less sharp, forgotten joy and woe,
Bright faces of the dead in youth, his playmates long ago,
Each bitter surge of wounded pride, each throb of childish
    pain,
Slight memories which he never thought to clothe with life
    again,
Streamed upward from his deepest heart, each scene a vivid
    whole,
As if some inner flash lit up the temple of the soul.
Then whilst these phantoms round him roamed, he knew
    not how or whence,
A keen and tingling clearness burnt along each aching
    sense.
What sound is that, which pierces through the thunder and
    the rain?
Is it a nerve beneath his ear? a pulse within his brain?
"Wake, Caius Julius, wake!" he cries, "some hostile thing
    is near,
"The sacred geese are hissing loud, and clattering wings of
    fear."
His drowsy friend, with half-shut eyes, and lips that scarcely
    stirred,
Just murmured, "We have dogs to watch, wait till their
    bark is heard."
Then Manlius smiled in playful scorn: "Well canst thou
    fight and feed,

"But art not framed of stuff to save a people in its need."
Lightly he took his good sword down, on light step left the tent,
And, like a panther, glided on, still listening as he went;
He reached the edge of rock which rose sheer from the level ground,
And peered into the night spread out, like a dark sea, around;
The whirlwind thundered round his head, but, as its fury passed,
There seemed to thrill a clank of steel keen through the deep-mouthed blast;
He lay like death, with his whole soul intensely hearkening there,
But once again the gust roared round, and filled the echoing air;
Another lull: that rattling sure was steel that clashed and rung!
And on the strained ear low words crept, breathed in that hostile tongue,
Whilst, rolling towards the Roman tents, and billowing from below,
A blacker gloom within the gloom seemed to move up and grow;
Then when the thunder cloud once more poured forth its lurid light,
Out burst a rush of iron helms and faces ghastly white.
"What ho!" brave Manlius cried, "to arms, to arms, ye Romans all!

"Be swift as fire, if ye would save your country from the Gaul."
Then shrill the Tuscan trumpets blew, and fierce the fight began,
Huge stones and pillared walls crashed loud upon each Gallic clan,
Until with half their men struck down they turned and fled amain,
Nor checked their flying feet until they reached the city plain.
Then as the shouts of joy went round, said Caius Julius, "Hark!
"Brave Manlius listen, even now, our dogs begin to bark."
The hero answered with a smile, "Be still, ye howling crew,
"To curs that sleep so sound and deep small thanks indeed are due."

BALACLAVA.

Thin glancing threads of English horse,
   Why do your haughty trumpets wake?
Through yon gray myriads, massed in force,
   None but the mad could hope to break!

" Men may be mad, or men be wise,
" But not with us the question lies;
" Although we guess not their intent,
  " This one thing well, we know,
" That, where the Light Brigade is sent,
   " The Light Brigade will go."
      What need to tell
      Of splintering shell,
Of cannon shot, and rifle-ball?
The death-hail smites them, one and all,
Through smoke that wraps them like a pall,
As raindrops, each on each, they fall.
     Horse rolls o'er horse,
     Corse hideth corse,
  The gaps grow wide, and wider,
     Deep-wounded men
     Crawl back agen;
Steeds rush without a rider:

BALACLAVA.

But still against the wondering foe,
In stubborn silence forward go
Unchecked, unslackening, undismayed,
The living of the Light Brigade,
Till that wild onset overbears
The guns in front, one moment theirs.
Sudden and sharp the halt is made,
   They seem, in mute reproach, to say,
"Your orders have been now obeyed,
   "As far as in us lay;
"Yours are these guns, with life-blood red,
"But can ye hold them by the dead?"
Meanwhile the cannon, from each hill,
Keep showering slaughter on them still,
   All paths with death are lined;
Dense columns bar their onward course,
And long blue streaks of Russian horse,
   Like nets, are spread behind.
That shattered remnant pauses there,
   Blown chargers, wounded men:
Oh! they will break, like yielding air,
   And who shall blame them then?
Not so—through that bewildered throng
Like fire the leaders glance along
From rank to rank; too far to hear,
We seem to feel an English cheer;
Whilst Fancy, from each blade waved high,
Each gesture fierce, and flashing eye,
Can proud words, such as these, supply:—

"Gather ye, gather ye, close up once more!
"Swords red to the wristband, hearts steel to the core,
"Lance, sabre, and carbine, dragoon and Cossack,
"Are strong to the sight, but they dare not attack;
"No cutting, give point, were they twenty to one,
"Men who wait to be charged, when we gallop, will run!"
They gather, they gather, they close up once more,
Swords red to the wristband, hearts steel to the core,
Though wide wounds may weaken, though horses may blow,
They have pace enough left for a dash at the foe;
Then, as hawks might swoop down through the toils of a
    spider,
Right at the blue line goes each horse and his rider.
It is rent like a rag, burst like bubbles asunder,
Whilst down from each height roars redoubled the thunder;
Still unstayed and unbroken, they cut their way through,
Past spears that outflank them, from swords that pursue.
With cannon and riflemen hot on their track,
Destroyed, but unconquered, we welcome them back:
Not a man in that death-charge his chief hath forsaken,
And the guns which ye flung them at—were they not taken?

    And though, beneath yon fatal hill,
        Their dead the valley strew,
    Grimly, with cold hands, clutching still
        The broken swords they drew,
    We will not call their lives ill spent,
        If, to all time, they show,
    That where the Light Brigade was sent,
        The Light Brigade would go.

LINES TO HELEN,

ON SENDING HER SOME FLOWERS FOR HER BIRTHDAY IN WINTER.

BENEATH the ray, belovèd one,
   Of those soft-shining eyes,
These orphan children of the sun
   Seek shelter from the skies.

To nestle at thy side they creep,
   (Young sunny-hearted thing!)
That on their dreaming buds, may sleep
   A shadow of the spring.

Yes! thou in this chill time wert born,
   To lend its darksome hours
The tender brightness of May-morn,
   A prophetess of flowers.

They drink that clear unclouded smile,
   Like genial light from heaven,
Receiving from thee, all the while,
   Far more than they have given.

They give but blooms which vanish soon,
   But fragrance, swift to die,
And Love repays the fleeting boon
   With immortality;

Of thy sweet image once a part,
   Its magic life they share,
And, rooted in one steadfast heart—
   They will not wither there.

I SAW HER LAST.

> Elle étoit de ce monde où les plus belles choses
>   Ont le pire destin ;
> Elle vecut, ce que vivent les roses,
>   L'espace d'un matin.

I saw her last, when love's warm light
    Lay deep within her modest eye,
When all futurity was bright
    Before her, like a summer sky—
It quieted both pain and fear,
To see a thing so happy near.

Yet was this blessedness a flower
    Too delicate for earth—alas !
Its leaves were withered in an hour ;
    As sunshine glideth from the grass,
And melts invisibly away,
So did she vanish from the day.

Then came soft sorrow upon all,
    That one so full of gentle grace

Beneath so rude a touch should fall;
   By eyes, that never saw her face,
Tears from the inmost heart were shed,
And all the happy mourned the dead:

They mourned her as the beautiful,
   Even as we mourn the rose's doom,
When every crimson leaf grows dull,
   And death feeds on the damask bloom;
They mourned her as she was—but I
Looked to our vanished infancy—
To those deep memories which seem
The very fountains of the stream.
The early unforgotten things
To which the spirit ever clings,
And feels throughout all change to be
The seal of her identity.
With the same blood our veins were rife,
The selfsame summer gave us life,
And this was as a silken tie
Of fellowship and sympathy—
Therefore, through childhood's sunny weather,
We were, as loving twins, together;
Together in the greenwood shade,
Day after day we laughed and played;
Together, with hushed breath, drew nigh
To snare the crimson butterfly,
Or stopped to hear the throstle sing
Beneath the mellow evening.

I SAW HER LAST.

Alas! how vain the hope I cherished,
That though the childish joys had perished,
The memory of these pleasant things
Would lend the weary spirit wings,
To flee away from care and sadness,
    From life's great sea of tossing foam,
From manhood's grief and manhood's gladness,
    Back to her youthful home.
Alas! that sunny place is not,
A cloud has deepened o'er the spot,
So that whene'er I summon back
The faded hues of childhood's track,
There comes upon me a distress,
A sense of solemn loneliness,
Which makes my spirit for a time
Shrink from that bright and blessèd clime,
To find a home in future things,
For the deep heart's imaginings;
Since she, who shared the past with me,
Has put on immortality.

THE SAVING OF THE COLOURS.

"In their death they were not divided."

"For victory!—no, all hope is gone; for life!—let that go too;
"But for the Colours still work on—the chance is left with you.
"I know to share our death with us ye both desire to stay,
"But these are my last orders—Mount! and with them force your way."

On Coghill and on Melvill thus these last commands were laid;
They left the Colonel where he stood, and without words obeyed.
In silence, then, that steadfast pair moved onward side by side,
And lifting with its staff the Flag, began their ghastly ride.

Watched through that wild and whirling fight, through wreaths of eddying smoke,
Their horses ridden hard and straight, on those bold foemen broke;

THE SAVING OF THE COLOURS.

Amid the dark lines plunging deep, their blades flashed
    back the light,
And then, like divers in the sea, they both are hid from sight.

But now we know they died not there, for rising up once
    more,
Through the rough battle-tide they beat, alive, though
    wounded sore;
The red drops fell like falling rain, but still their steeds
    were swift;
And hope is strong within them as they gallop for the Drift.

O'er grinning boulders guided safe, forced through fierce
    tufts of thorn,
Then dashing like a torrent down the path by torrents
    worn;
Well handled in that fearful race, and never slackening
    speed,
The chargers struggle gallantly, nor fail them at their need.

In vain the dusky giants spread all over that rough ground;
With cruel eyes and glistering teeth, like panthers leap around;
Melvill's skilled bridle-hand is there, and Coghill's hovering
    sword;
A new escape each stride, but still, they foil that furious
    horde.

Till, toiling through the reed-beds dank, and up the wild
    ravine,

They gain the open hill-top whence the longed-for Drift is seen.
Alas! the rifles flash and ring—alas! like billows roll
Besieging masses to and fro, between them and their goal.

The last frail chance they feel is gone, and turn at once aside:
But turn without despairing, since not for themselves they ride.
Beyond the flood, a furlong's breadth, the land is English land,
And they must bear our Colours there, though in a dying hand.

They plunge and swim, the stream runs on—runs dark with priceless gore,
But that high purpose in the heart lends life, and something more;
For though their best blood mingle with the rain-swelled river's foam,
Death has no power to stop them till they bring their Colours home.

Death had not power to stop them. No! when through spates rolling dim,
Melvill, half-drowned, cried out aloud to help the Flag—not him;
When Coghill, crippled and outworn, retreading that grim track,
A martyr in war's noble faith, to certain fate rode back——

They had, it might be thought, to die, leaving their work
    half done,
But aids unseen rose up to end the task so well begun :
It was as if the intense desire through earth, air, water
    wrought,
Passed from them with their passing souls, and home the
    Colours brought.

Those Colours, saved for happier days, and armed with that
    desire,
Shall feel the last breath of the dead thrill through their
    folds like fire;
And by the spirit-memories of that bold ride made strong,
O'er many a battlefield in power shall yet be borne along.

But those who shielded them from shame, and through
    fierce thousands made
A passage for them with their blood, are in one silence laid ;
Silence between the strife and them, between them and the
    cheers
That greet the Flag returning slow, the welcome and the
    tears.

For now, forgetting that wild ride, forgetful of all pain,
High amongst those who have not lived, who have not
    died in vain,
By strange stars watched, they sleep afar, within some
    nameless glen,
Beyond the tumult and the noise, beyond the praise of men.

But we who feel what wealth of hope for ever there was lost,
What bitter sorrow burns for them, how dear those Colours cost,
Can but recall the sad old truth, so often said and sung,
That brightest lives fade first—that those whom the gods love die young.

THE FOSTER BROTHER.

FROM M. DE VILLEMARQUÉ'S *BRETON BALLADS*.

This ballad, in point of conception, seems to me to indicate greater subtlety and delicacy of imagination than Bürger's "Wilhelm and Leonora," which is, apparently, another form of the same tradition. What may be the history of the German poem—familiar to all English readers through the translations of Scott, Spencer, etc.—I do not know, but it has apparently been modernised by some one, and adapted, very crudely, I think, to a Christian audience. The Breton minstrels, on the other hand, have transmitted the old lay just as it came down to them, without troubling themselves to consider that the Island of the Blest, where youths and maidens, amid golden-fruited orchards, dance for ever on the banks of crystal streams, sparkling in eternal sunshine, has more in it of a pagan elysium than of a mediæval Christian heaven. The result of this is, unless I am deceived, that their poem is more completely in harmony with itself, and more satisfactory to the reader or hearer, than that of their rival. The German catastrophe—which probably was at one time the same, more or less, as that of the following ballad—has now, in consequence of the monkish or Lutheran dislocation of its point of view, been made somewhat repulsive to the ordinary reader. We do not readily surrender a maiden, who is tender, passionate, and true, to eternal and exceptional damnation, because she is tender, passionate, and true—even though, under the first pressure of grief, she may have shown herself, for a moment, less submissive to the will of God than is fitting. Moreover, the supernatural machinery of the Teuton is coarse as compared with that of the Celt. The German girl is carried off bodily by the devil, disguised as her lover. She is plunged into hell-fire, and no mistake, as a schoolboy would say. There are none of those whispered half-tones, or mysterious possibilities; none of those alternating lights and shadows which play round the imagination, and give double effect to anything like a ghost story, whether in prose or in verse. Now the touches of this kind in the Breton ballad are to me peculiarly happy. Who is that knight who rides fearlessly from Nantes through the river, haunted by the capricious and formidable dwarfs? He may be nothing more than a messenger from his wounded friend, indifferent to local superstitions, who takes the shortest road. And yet the suddenness of his appearance on that awful spot, and his accurate prediction of the exact time when the dying man will be sufficiently recovered to show himself in the same phantom-peopled place, "forbid us to interpret so." We are left in that twilight state of mind, when the unquiet shadow seems to become a distinct living shape, and the imagination passes into the blood; whereas, if we are told that the knight was simply a Corrigan, or Breton fairy, in disguise, we should passively acquiesce, and feel but little excitement in the matter. Again, when in the German ballad Leonora is carried off bodily, and does not reappear, we have to take it on the positive assertion of Mr. Bürger, that she is gone, body and soul, to hell. There is nothing for the fancy to work upon and brood over. Now with regard to Gwennolak, after the spectral ride is ended, her virgin corpse is found, but just where it would be found, if she had died of exhaustion and despair, in the delirium of brain fever. Was then that delicious gallop into Paradise, behind her devoted lover, the dream of a dying maniac, sent in mercy from heaven to wipe away the tears from her eyes, and smooth her passage from this rough world to a better, but still a dream? or was it a reality for the soul, unconscious, till the ride was over, that it had passed into the home of spirits? Considered as listeners, sitting under the singer, to use the accredited phrase, we believe it was. But the doubts and the various possibilities which arise kindle our imagination, and give our feelings and fancies an activity of their own from within, which, from my point of view, is the proper effect of a true poem. I repeat, therefore, what I said above, that this legend, probably one of great antiquity, has been preserved in a more poetical form by the Celt than by the Teuton.

THE FOSTER BROTHER.

No fairer maid throughout the land than Gwennolak was seen,
The daughter of a noble house, a maiden of eighteen.
Dead the old lord her father, dead two sisters, and her mother.
Her father's wife was left; but of her own blood breathed no other.
'Twas sad by that manorial hall, at the threshold of its door,
To see that young and gentle girl still weeping—weeping sore:
Her eyes look seaward for the ship of her foster brother dear,
Her life's one solace, waited for in hope this many a year.
Her eyes look seaward for the ship of that foster brother dear;
Six times hath opened since he went, six times hath closed, the year.

" Out of my path!" (the harsh one cried), " drive home at once the kine;
" 'Tis not to sit before me there I give thee food of mine."
Two hours—three hours—ere dawn, the fires to light, the house to sweep,
That woman used to rouse the girl, in winter dark and deep;
In pitcher cracked, or leaky pail, to bring them water back
From the stream, whence the wild dwarf-river rolls on its haunted track.

Black was the night; across the ford of that enchanted
 flood,
The horse-hoofs of a knight from Nantes trampled the
 stream to mud.
"Hail, fair one! art thou yet betrothed?"—a childish thing,
 and shy,
(These were her very words to us), "I cannot tell," said I.
"Nay, sweet one, art thou yet betrothed? Hide not the
 truth, I pray."
"Nay, by your leave, fair sir, not yet have I been given
 away."
"Take then this ring of gold, and tell thy father's wife, that
 thou
"To wed a knight who comes from Nantes hast pledged
 thy maiden vow.
"There mighty hath the battle been, there his young squire
 hath died:
"He, too, is sorely wounded by a sword-stroke in the side;
"Still, in three weeks and three days more, that wound will
 healèd be,
"And to the castle he will ride lightly, for love of thee."
Straight to the house she ran—meanwhile she looked upon
 the stone;
That signet-ring, she knows it is her foster brother's own.

One week went by, two weeks went by, three weeks went
 by, alack!
And still no brave young knight from Nantes comes lightly
 riding back.

Her father's wife said, "In my heart I've toiled and thought
 for thee;
"A fitting bridegroom I have found, and married shalt
 thou be."
"By your good leave, fair mother mine, no husband will I
 take,
"Save my own foster brother dear, who cometh for my sake.
"He gave me a gold ring to wear upon my wedding-day;
"And soon will come delightedly to carry me away."
"Silence about thy wedding-day, and thy gold ring so fine,
"Or I will teach thee how to talk—ay! with this staff of
 mine.
"It is with Jobig Allodok that ye to church must go—
"Jobig, our stable varlet young, whether you choose or no."
"With Jobig?—I shall die of grief!—oh, horrible!—my own
"Dear little mother, how couldst thou thus leave me here
 alone?"
"Off to the courtyard, and weep there. Go hence, and
 weep your fill.
"In three days you his bride shall be—his bride, pout as
 you will."

About that time the sexton old went round the country side,
Ringing his peal of death to tell of some one who had died.
"Pray for the soul that was but now a noble and a knight,
"Who, during life, with stainless heart, stood up for truth
 and right.
"Whilst mighty battle beyond Nantes was raging wild and
 wide,

"His death-wound from a sword-stroke came—a sword-stroke in the side.

"When sets to-morrow's sun, they will to watch his corpse begin;

"Then from the white church bear him down, to rest his grave within."

"You're early back." "In troth, am I; for I could bear no more:

"Not that the feast is ended yet, not that the night is o'er;

"But to behold that cowherd lout confronting them in hall

"Filled me with rage and pity, which I could not check at all.

"Around that hapless maid forlorn, whose salt tears never ceased,

"There sat no guest who did not weep, not e'en our aged priest.

"This morning in the parish church wept old and young; no eye,

"Saving her stepmother's alone, at the sad sight kept dry.

"The more the minstrels, coming home, their joy-bells clashed and swung,

"The more they tried to soothe her grief, the more her heart was wrung.

"At supper-time, poor child, when she to the high place was led,

"No drop of water could she drink, nor touch a crumb of bread.

" They would have then undressed her straight, in bridal
    bed to lay;
" She tore her marriage girdle off, and tossed her ring away.
" Forth from the house she rushed amain, with loosely
    floating hair,
" And now is hiding nigh at hand, no mortal knoweth
    where."

All lights were out within the tower, all slept in silence
    there,
Save that poor child, who watched apart, in a fever of
    despair.
" Who's there?"   " 'Tis I, my Nola sweet, your foster
    brother true!"
" You, brother of my heart?—Oh joy! Can it indeed be
    you?"
Straight leapt she on the milk-white steed, the steed her
    brother rode,
Close clung her slight arms from behind, as on the charger
    strode.
" How fast we go! we've ridden, love, a hundred leagues, I
    trow.
" I feel so happy with thee; ne'er have I been blest as
    now.
" But is thy mother's house far off?—would I were there at
    last."
" Anon! anon!—only do thou, sweet sister, hold me fast."
As on they rode, the owl, in front, fled hooting down the
    glade;

The wild beasts of the wood dashed off, scared at the sound they made.

"How lithe thy steed! thy coat of mail, how richly doth it shine!

"How thou art grown since last we met, dear foster brother mine!

"How fair thou art to look on! Still, is thy home distant? Say."

"Ere long we shall be there, do thou but hold me firm alway."

"Thy heart is ice, thy hair feels damp—hand, heart, are ice alike.

"Thou'rt cold, I fear, for from thy heart the death-chills on me strike."

"Still hold thee fast, my sister sweet; we now are close at hand.

"Dost thou not hear the ringing tunes of our blithe wedding band?"

He scarce had spoken, when at once that headlong course was stayed;

The proud steed shivered where he stood, then mightily he neighed.

They found themselves within an isle; there folks were dancing gay;

There, hand in hand, fair maids and youths wheeled round in happy play;

There bright-hued trees grew all around, which golden fruitage bore;

Behind glowed sunrise on the hills—it rose to set no more.

Down from those peaks a fountain poured its bright stream through the plain;
All souls that of that water drink come back to life again.
There Nola's mother smiled once more, both sisters at her side;
There pleasure never failed, and song to shouts of joy replied.

When next on earth day dawned, young maids, arrayed in robes of gloom,
Bore little Nola's spotless form from the white church to the tomb.

THE LOSS OF THE "BIRKENHEAD."

SUPPOSED TO BE TOLD BY A SOLDIER WHO SURVIVED.

RIGHT on our flank the sun was dropping down;
    The deep sea heaved around in bright repose;
When, like the wild shriek from some captured town,
        A cry of women rose.

The stout ship "Birkenhead" lay hard and fast,
    Caught without hope upon a hidden rock;
Her timbers thrilled as nerves, when thro' them passed
        The spirit of that shock.

And ever like base cowards, who leave their ranks
    In danger's hour, before the rush of steel,
Drifted away, disorderly, the planks
        From underneath her keel.

So calm the air—so calm and still the flood,
    That low down in its blue translucent glass
We saw the great fierce fish, that thirst for blood,
        Pass slowly, then repass.

They tarried, the waves tarried, for their prey!
   The sea turned one clear smile! Like things asleep
Those dark shapes in the azure silence lay,
      As quiet as the deep.

Then amidst oath, and prayer, and rush, and wreck,
   Faint screams, faint questions waiting no reply,
Our Colonel gave the word, and on the deck
      Form'd us in line to die.

To die!—'twas hard, while the sleek ocean glow'd
   Beneath a sky as fair as summer flowers:—
All to the boats! cried one—he was, thank God,
      No officer of ours.

Our English hearts beat true—we would not stir:
   That base appeal we heard, but heeded not:
On land, on sea, we had our Colours, sir,
      To keep without a spot.

They shall not say in England, that we fought
   With shameful strength, unhonour'd life to seek;
Into mean safety, mean deserters, brought
      By trampling down the weak.

So we made women with their children go,
   The oars ply back again, and yet again;
Whilst, inch by inch, the drowning ship sank low,
      Still, under steadfast men.

——What follows, why recall?—The brave who died,
    Died without flinching in the bloody surf,
They sleep as well beneath that purple tide
        As others under turf.

They sleep as well! and, roused from their wild grave,
    Wearing their wounds like stars, shall rise again,
Joint-heirs with Christ, because they bled to save
        His weak ones, not in vain.

If that day's work no clasp or medal mark;
    If each proud heart no cross of bronze may press,
Nor cannon thunder loud from Tower or Park,
        This feel we none the less:—

That those whom God's high grace there saved from ill,
    Those also left His martyrs in the bay,
Though not by siege, though not in battle, still
        Full well had earned their pay.

VERSES WRITTEN FOR MUSIC.

Like to the moan of buried rivers,
    Heard faintly, as they roam,
Whilst the wild rock around them shivers
    Through sheets of sunless foam;
Beneath the life that weighs and presses,
    With muffled undertone,
Throbs, in the spirit's worn recesses,
    The voice of years long flown.

If, in the tumult of existence,
    It whisper soft and low,
Yea seem, scarce heard through depths of distance,
    To melt away and go:
Yet oft, when stars more whitely glitter,
    When moons are waning chill,
That tide unseen grows loud and bitter,
    The caverned heart to fill.

And as the other night, unbroken,
    And starless, hangs around,

Old words, half thought, old thoughts, half spoken,
    Pour in to swell the sound.
Though Death's dumb frost all else is hushing,
    From that undying past,
The voice not lost, the stream, still rushing,
    Shall murmur to the last.

SEQUEL TO THE ABOVE.

WRITTEN for music, still the words are young,
    The notes that met them full of life remain,
But where is she from whose clear spirit sprung
       Their melody in vain?

Where is the fair young wife, so dear to all,
    Who, flushed with hope, like some half-opening flower,
Felt all her heart awaken at Love's call,
       And blossom into power?

Sometimes she even deemed it new delight
    To play with sorrow, as the sun of June
Plays with a cloud, self-veiled, to issue bright
       In double glory, soon.

Therefore, whilst asking me for song, she bade
    That wailing words, to wailing music set,
Should glide, like forest-streams, beneath a shade,
       And murmur of regret.

SEQUEL TO THE ABOVE.

Through buried hours I dived to depths where low
    Down in the vaults and windings of the soul,
Faint echoes of each half-forgotten woe,
      Like distant death-bells, toll.

As their dumb moanings grew to speech, I said,
    Said, not ill-pleased, "Though I no longer hear,
"Still shall these thoughts of mine to song be wed,
      "Through many a golden year;

"Still shall this joyous creature, as beseems
    "Young beauty, shine in her appointed place,
"Like spring enriching that old hall, with gleams
      "Of genius, love, and grace."

Not such His will on high; He leaves the old
    As oaks outlive bright roses, in the gloom
Of winter crawling onward, to behold
      Grim Nature's waste of bloom.

Her earthly songs are sung, her tale is told;
    She rests where burn soft lamps, by memory fed,
Through haunted galleries of the heart, which hold
      Pale pictures of the dead;

Pale pictures, in whose visionary eyes
    Lost smiles live on, and phantom laughter plays;
From whose weird lips, with wordless utterance, rise
      The tones of other days.

And thus not wholly claimed by God; for him
    To whom her maiden faith and love were given,
The tender shadows of that face make dim
    All light, but light from heaven.

And the sweet voice, grown sweeter yet, through death
    Steals whispering round her children from above,
To fill their orphan dreamings with the breath
    Of some diviner love.

SHORT ANALYSIS OF THE "PLURALITY OF WORLDS."

SHOULD man, through the stars, to far galaxies travel,
And of nebulous films the remotest unravel,
He still could but learn, having fathomed infinity,
That the great work of God was—The Master of Trinity.

AN EPITAPH IN COBHAM CHURCHYARD TURNED INTO VERSE.

THE marble of this massive Tomb
Weighs down the bones of H. . . . y C. . . . e ;
If faults he had, in civic shocks,
At least he stood by Charles James Fox,
And rather would his throat have slit
Than given a cheer for Billy Pitt.
Therefore, ye liberal Angels, haste and chair him
   As a stout Partisan, and true—
And to "The First Great Whig" in triumph bear him,
   On pinions sulphur-buff and blue.

EPITAPH ON A FAVOURITE DOG.

NOT hopeless, round this calm sepulchral spot,
   A wreath, presaging life, we twine;
If God be love, what sleeps below was not
   Without a spark divine.

ODE FOR MUSIC.

TO BE SUNG IN THE SHELDONIAN THEATRE, OXFORD,

AT THE ENCÆNIA, JUNE 1870

ON THE FIRST VISIT OF THE MOST HON. THE MARQUIS OF
SALISBURY, CHANCELLOR.

Now let us praise our famous men,
   With melodies, whose eager flight
   Throbs through the trembling air as light,
With all that blended influence, when
   Sweet harp-like voices thrill around,
   Above the organ's thunder sound,
Die faintly off, then soar agen :
So let us praise our famous men.

As lulled by each mysterious note,
   On vanished hopes and hours we dwell,
Low murmurs through the music float,
   As of some murmuring ocean shell.
From the pale distance of the dead
   A faint breath wavers to and fro,
Like unforgotten fragrance shed
   On May morns long ago.

Oxford, full many a child of thine,
    We yearn for now with hearts forlorn,
Who poured away fresh youth, like wine,
    And sunk, with noble toils outworn.
Unchanging now, by day or night,
    Before these dim and agèd eyes,
For ever young, for ever bright,
    Our early lost arise.

Herbert, the loved of all, whose smile
    Upon each memory lingers yet,
Like sunlight, hovering for a while
    After the sun himself hath set.
Elgin, who held his life alway
    A thing to spend for England's use;
Who left in death another ray
    Round the proud name of Bruce.

Lewis, the calm and just; he too,
    Through Fate's dark void has passed afar,
Unselfish, loyal, wise, and true,
    And stainless ever as a star.
Last that great sire's great son,[1] who when
    The steams of blood choked Indian air,
And fear made others cruel, then
    Rose strong enough to spare.

[1] Lord Canning.

Now full of hope, though sad, we meet
    The silent place of one to fill;
Whose knightly heart has ceased to beat,
    Whose silver voice for earth is still;
Our Derby, to new work gone forth,
    We here must honour as we can:
But grateful toilers of the North [1]
    Praise best that famous man.

Hard is the task for those who seek
    A coming age to shape, like thee;
Still, Cecil, if the soul grow weak,
    Look back, look back, in faith, and see
How amid threatening clouds, which hung
    Erewhile around each honoured name,
On the storm's very heart were flung
    The rainbow lights of fame.

In these uncertain hours, when gloom
    Walls the weird Future from our eyes,
And Time, before his wavering loom,
    Steeps the dim thread in sullen dyes;
Although for us, harsh Fate may will
    To blight the years not yet unrolled;
Nor man, nor God, hath power to kill
    The hero-work of old.

---

[1] Alluding to the late Lord Derby's exertions during the Lancashire cotton famine.

The fathers of our ancient race,
    Together—not their chiefs alone—
Strong, each in his appointed place,
    Have made a matchless Past our own;
Must these proud memories fail and sink,
    Like white sparks flashing on the shore?
Or will God's hand shine out, and link
    Heart unto heart once more?

When Spain's insulting keels essayed
    To crush the soul of our wild sea,
Even as her brooding power had weighed
    Upon the spirits of the free;
Time tells us how the people rose,
    Like tides, onsweeping in their flow
To lift the great as foam, that shows
    An ocean's strength below.

Then moved thy sire, in light above
    The mighty wave of England's heart:
One with it—resting on its love;
    Too wise to dream of life apart.
Danger frowns near, and must be met;
    We may be called to front again
A tyranny more baleful yet,
    A deadlier foe, than Spain.

The stealthy tread of hate and greed,
    How it creeps on half heard, we feel;

Yet trifle still, and take no heed
    Of smilers whetting hidden steel.
When the war leaps on us at length,
    From silence, and without a sign;
To whom should England turn for strength,
    If not to Burleigh's line?

He, 'gainst the rush of peril, showed
    Fresh courage as the foe drew nigher,
And fused men's thoughts, until they glowed,
    Like one great breath of living fire.
Seek thou, as he sought, to uplift
    To her old height our English soul;
To heal each wound, to close each rift,
    To make our armour whole.

So shalt thou face the struggle stern,
    That lies before thee on thy way;
And victor thus, or vanquished, earn
    A wreath more lasting than the bay.
So shalt thou find that other feet
    Tread other paths, to the same end;
And under one high influence, greet
    Each true man as a friend.

To sow, for years remote, the seed
    Of knowledge—soothe intestine strife;
To cheer the land with hope, to feed,
    And guide, not quench, the fires of life;

To serve untired, whate'er befall,
    To save, renew, create, unfold;
Is not this work that claimeth all?
    For wise the words of old;

Easy, indeed, to shake a state;[1]
    That much at least may do
Some slight and worthless man, but great
    And tasking wrestlers' limbs, the feat
To fix her in her former seat,
    And build the whole anew.

Yea, tasking sinew, brain, and soul,
    From harm the ancient fane to keep,
Whilst overhead harsh thunders roll,
    And outbursts billowing from below,
    The deepset earth whirl to and fro.

The dead have done their work, they sleep,
    Safe from all chance of ill;
But yet, unfaltering in its flight,
    From their cold hands with fiery leap,
Before the breath of God's high will,
    The torch of Fate right onward runs,
    And England calls her living sons,
Ere they are left alone with night,
To grasp and raise that quenchless light.

[1] Pindar, 4th Pythian.

She calls on each with ill to cope,
Mailed in bright aims and self-less hope,
To thrust all meaner lusts aside,
And love his country as a bride;
So all the good, for her dear sake,
   Close joining hand to hand,
Shall of one glorious toil partake,
   Till peace hath filled the land.

Hence, whilst we praise our famous men,
   With melodies, whose eager flight
   Throbs through the living air, as light,
With all that music lendeth, when
   Sweet harp-like voices thrill around,
   Above the organ's thunder-sound,
Dreamlike die off, then soar again—
Thy name shall sound among them then.

THE QUICK MARCH OF THE FOURTEENTH REGIMENT.

[On May 23, 1793, my grandfather Welbore Ellis Doyle rallied his regiment—the 14th of the Line—then wavering under a heavy fire, and stormed the fortified camp of Famars, after a very severe action, to the tune of *Ça Ira*. For many years this tune continued to be the quick march of the 14th Regiment. I understand that of late years the tradition has ceased to operate, and that the march is disused, or, at least, that its origin has been forgotten.]

WHEN first the might of France was set
'Gainst creeds and laws, long years ago,
And the great strife—not ended yet—
Tossed crowns and nations to and fro,
Now buried deep beneath those wars
That since have made the earth their prey,
Our hard-won triumph at Famars
Was famous in its day.

Here—trained through steadfast work, and drilled
Till as one thought they moved along,
By the old land's old memories filled,
Our English lads were calm and strong.

There—drunk on hope as on new wine,
That in their veins like madness wrought,
With power half-devilish, half-divine,
Each restless Frenchman fought.

Wealth, numbers, skill they heeded not,
Trampling them down as common things;
Man's spirit was a fire, made hot
To burn away the strength of kings.
Thus armed, as roars before the blast,
At forest trees a prairie flame,
On our firm silence, fiercely fast,
Their howling frenzy came—

Until (why shun the truth to speak?)
The courage rooted in the past
Struck, as by sudden storms, grew weak,
And wavered like a wavering mast:
Still kept their time the well-taught feet,
Nor dreamed the soldier yet of flight,
Though deepening shadows of defeat
Fell on him, like a blight.

Straight out in front their leader dashed
(A God-given king of men was he),
And from his bright looks on them flashed
One sparkle of heroic glee:

T

"They hold us cheap" (he cried) "too soon,
"We'll break them, frantic as they are,
"Unto their own accursèd tune;
"Strike up then *Ça Ira*."

The drums exulting thundered forth,
Whilst yet with trumpet tones he spoke,
And in those strong sons of the North
The old Berserker laugh awoke.
Their bayonets glowed with life, their eyes
Shone out to greet that eagle glance,
And, in her rush, a strange surprise
Palsied the steps of France.

Then, like a stream that bursts its banks,[1]
To *Ça Ira* from fifes and drums,
Upon their crushed and shattered ranks
The cataract charge of England comes;
Whilst their own conquering music leapt
Forth in wild mirth to feel them run;
Right o'er the ridge that host was swept,
And the grim battle won.

Thus, in the face of heaven and earth,
From their first home those notes he tore
To live, as by a second birth,
Linked fast with England evermore.

---

[1] This line is from *Rokeby*. I borrowed it unconsciously at the moment, and thought afterwards that Scott was quite rich enough to lend it to me without feeling the loss.

Yes, evermore, that through them still
To coming ages might be shown,
Whose arrowy thought and iron will
Had made that prize his own.

Thence, as each panting year rushed by
With garments rolled in blood—His march
Went sounding onwards, far and nigh—
Beneath cold rains, or suns that parch,
Northward or southward—east or west,
Where still the heirs of that renown,
Behind some other colonel, pressed
To the field hurrying down.

For him, alas! on Java's shore
It throbbed unheard through purple skies,
Nor marked he, under dark Bhurtpore,
The blood-bought battle-hymn arise.
New Zealand's fern-gloom, as they stept,
Might quiver to that piercing tone,
But him it stirred not, where he slept
In a far land—alone.

And, whilst o'er its old ground, the strain
Smote with high scorn our ancient foe,
Called he upon those drums again?
Shared he their closing rapture? No!

His grave lay deep in dust, before
They pealed through Belgian corn-crops, when
The baffled Eagle fell, no more
To tear the hearts of men.

Yes, he died young, and all in vain
We dream how much he left undone,
Painting, upon an idle brain,
The glorious course he should have run.
Forgotten by the reckless years,
He rests apart—and makes no sign—
Even his proud march no longer cheers
The Fourteenth of the Line.

Still, if elsewhere of this no trace
Remain, by some as worthy deed,
Oh, youthful soldiers of his race,
Against oblivion for it plead.
Thus, if his death-lamp have grown dim,
Re-light it; thus force Time to spare
This leaf of laurel, earned by him
For the old name we bear.

IPHITION.

> Ἐν δ' Ἀχιλεὺς Τρώεσσι θόρε, . . .
> σμερδαλέα ἰάχων· πρῶτον δ' ἕλεν Ἰφιτίωνα
> . . . . .
> τὸν δ' ἰθὺς μεμαῶτα βάλ' ἔγχεϊ δῖος Ἀχιλλεύς,
> μέσσην κὰκ κεφαλήν.—*Iliad,* xx. 381, κ.τ.λ.

How, facing an unconquerable foe
   Silent and firm in the lost battle's roar,
Iphition fell, three thousand years ago,
   We learn ;—let him have praise for evermore.

What! though his slayer, drunk with Eastern blood,
   Be borne aloft on wider wings of fame,
Two words, by Homer dropped in careless mood,
   Give light enough to read a hero's name.

The shout that shattered armies into flight,
   The godlike form in heaven's own armour clad,
The golden plumes divine that lived with light
   At every step, for him no terrors had.

Right on he rushed, though to a certain doom,
    Hephæstian mail and matchless strength defied;
And, carrying with him proudly to the tomb
    The whiteness of his honour, so he died.

There Homer leaves him, like a tall ship wrecked—
    Leaves him to wolves and vultures where he lay;
But that which makes the man, no bard's neglect
    To beast, or bird, or Time can yield a prey.

Thus ever, through Eternity, we dream
    That he by looking back is comforted,
That the long sunless hours of Hades gleam,
    With radiance from the past around him shed;

That inward still he murmurs, as the wind
    Murmurs through roofless halls: "At least I know
None find a spot in my young life behind,
    Nor dread I here what all must undergo.

" Death cometh—ay! but after death to say
    " What I with truth *can* say is given to few.
" Achilles, thine the fame—yet well I may
    " Believe myself the better of the two.

" Armed by no god, but as my fellow-men,
    " I faltered not in fight, though others fled,
" Till my safe conqueror struck me down, and then
    " Against his lance, the blood leapt warm and red.

" And even here, on this unhoping coast,
  " With spirit unexhausted I can bow
" To what Fate sends; Achilles, as a ghost,
  " Whines, weak without his god-given armour now.

" Though what life lent my soul no longer aid;
  " The memory that I never quailed, for me
" Keeps vital warmth within. I scorn the shade
  " That, to touch earth again, a slave would be."[1]

[1] *Odyssey*, b. xi. 488-90.

DARKNESS AND LIGHT.

We stood in silence, weak, and worn, and hapless,
   With Death's pale coming seen at length by all;
Whilst withered hopes beneath our feet lay sapless,
      Like leaves that fall.

But, as a fair girl through an opening door,
   Smiles on her father's servant, who has come
From wearying tasks, and pastimes prized no more,
      To bear her home—

So upon Death our dying maiden smiled;
   Then laid her head upon that Father's breast,
And sank, as sinks at eve a happy child,
      Into sweet rest.

Then, though to me that night of bitter pain
   Kept whispering through its frozen gloom, "Why stop
" For sorrow? life, too heavy to sustain,
      " May be let drop."

And through the vigil, desolate and drear,
   Vainly I listened, vainly looked, to find
Some voice beyond the void, some ray to cheer
      That darkness blind.

Yet deem I not that God remained apart;
   Though I saw nought, nor heard the sound of speech,
Yet he drew near, and pitied the dead heart
      He could not reach.

For in those hours, by His especial grace,
   Peace came to one pure breast then wounded sore,
And in a dream—not all a dream—that face
      Was seen once more.

Straight, o'er her sleeping sister's head, the blue—
   The chill deceiving blue—called heaven was rent,
And other Heavens within, divinely true,
      To sight were lent.

And there, but not alone, our lost one knelt;
   Before her mother bent in sweet surprise,
She seemed to whisper all she feared and felt,
      Beneath soft eyes.

Just so she looked of old to that fond mother
   Confessing some child-fault of days gone by;
One angel arm shone round her thrown, the other
      Was raised on high,

And pointed to a light that burned above,
　　Immeasurably distant—but yet near;
Radiant though soft, the perfect light of love
　　Which casts out fear.

Thus from those presences a blessing fell,
　　First on the sorrowing girl, direct from Heaven,
Thence, even to me, because I too loved well,
　　Through her was given.

SECRET AFFINITIES.

A PANTHEISTIC FANTASY, FROM THE FRENCH OF
THÉOPHILE GAUTIER.

DEEP in the vanished time, two statues white,
  On an old temple's front, against blue gleams
Of an Athenian sky, instinct with light,
  Blended their marble dreams.

In the same shell imbedded (crystal tears
  Of the sad sea mourning her Venus flown),
Two pearls of loneliest ocean, through long years,
  Kept whispering words unknown.

In the fresh pleasaunce, by Grenada's river,
  Close to the low-voiced fountain's silver showers,
Two roses, from Boabdil's garden, ever
  Mingled their murmuring flowers.

Upon the domes of Venice, in a nest
  Where love from age to age has had his day,
Two white doves, with their feet of pink, found rest
  Through the soft month of May.

Dove, rose, pearl, marble, into ruin dim
    Alike dissolve themselves, alike decay;
Pearls melt, flowers wither, marble shapes dislimn,
    And bright birds float away.

Each element, once free, flies back to feed
    The unfathomable Life-dust, yearning dumb,
Whence God's all-shaping hands in silence knead
    Each form that is to come.

By slow, slow change, to white and tender flesh
    The marble softens down its flawless grain;
The rose, in lips as sweet and red and fresh
    Refigured, blooms again.

Once more the doves murmur and coo beneath
    The hearts of two young lovers, when they meet;
The pearls renew themselves, and flash as teeth
    Through smiles divinely sweet.

Hence sympathetic emanations flow,
    And with soft tyranny the heart controul;
Touched by them, kindred spirits learn to know
    Their sisterhood of soul.

Obedient to the hint some fragrance sends,
    Some colour, or some ray with mystic power,
Atom to atom never swerving tends,
    As the bee seeks her flower.

Of moonlight visions round the temple shed,
   Of lives linked in the sea, a memory wakes,
Of flower-talk flushing through the petals red
   Where the bright fountain breaks.

Kisses, and wings that shivered to the kiss,
   On golden domes afar, come back to rain
Sweet influence; faithful to remembered bliss,
   The old love stirs again.

Forgotten presences shine forth, the past
   Is for the visionary eye unsealed;
The breathing flower, in crimson lips recast,
   Lives to herself revealed.

Where the laugh plays a glittering mouth within
   The pearl reclaims her lustre softly bright;
The marble throbs, fused in a maiden skin
   As fresh, and pure, and white.

Under some low and gentle voice the dove
   Has found an echo of her tender moan;
Resistance grows impossible, and love
   Springs up from the unknown.

Oh! thou whom burning, trembling, I adore,
   What shrine, what sea, what dome, what rose-tree bower,
Saw us, as mingling marble, joined of yore,
   Or pearl, or bird, or flower?

THE FOUNTAIN.

FROM THE FRENCH OF THÉOPHILE GAUTIER.

A FOUNTAIN bubbles forth, hard by the lake,
   Between two stones up-sparkling ever,
And merrily their course the waters take,
   As if to launch some famous river.

Softly she murmurs, "What delight is mine!
   " It was so cold and dark below;
" But now my banks green in the sunlight shine,
   " Bright skies upon my mirror glow;

" The blue forget-me-nots through tender sighs,
   " ' Remember us,' keep ever saying;
" On a strong wing the gem-like dragon-flies
   " Ruffle me, as they sweep round playing.

" The bird drinks at my cup; and now who knows
   " After this rush through grass and flowers,
" I may become a giant stream, that flows
   " Past rocks and valleys, woods and towers.

" My foam may lie, a lace-like fringe, upon
   " Bridges of stone, and granite quays,
" And bear the smoking steam-ship on, and on,
   " To earth-embracing seas."

Thus the young rivulet prattled as it went,
   With countless hopes and fancies fraught;
Like boiling water in a vessel pent,
   Throbbed through its bed the imprisoned thought.

But close upon the cradle frowns the tomb;
   A babe the future Titan dies,
For in the near lake's gulph of azure gloom
   The scarce-born fountain buried lies.

AT SEA.

1880.

"There was silence in heaven about the space of half an hour."
REV. viii. 1.

OLD Ocean rolls like time, each billow passing
Into another melts, and is no more,
Whilst the indwelling spirit works on, massing
   The great whole as before.

The separate waves are swift to come and go,
But the deep smiles, as they die one by one,
In lazy pleasure lifting from below
   His foam-flecked purple to the sun.

Eve comes, the floods race past, we see their white
Thrilled through by weird sea-fires, a burning shiver
Which for one moment lives in eager light
   And then—is quenched for ever.

Even so, alas, the bright chiefs of our race,
Lost under the interminable years,
Homer, or Shakspeare—each in his own place,
   Just flashes forth, then disappears;

For what we call their Immortality
Is a brief spark, born but to be destroyed,
As the long ruin of all things that be
   Moves down the Godless void.

Such is the creed our wise ones of the earth
Engrave now on the slowly-waning skies;
Ice, night, and death—death with no second birth—
   Even now before their prescient eyes,

Pale in the lone abysses of existence,
World hangs on world, system on system, dead,
Whilst over all out-wearied life's resistance
   Vast wings of blackness spread;

Till that proud voice, "Let there be light," whose breath
Came, as we deemed, from Heaven old glooms to chase,
Hath passed unfelt through a dim waste of death,
   To cease at length upon deaf space.

Darkness, eternal darkness, darkness bare
Of warmth, of life, of thought, with orbs that run,
Like sad ghosts of the shining years that were,
   Each round its frozen sun.

Sages may scoff, "What matters this to you
"Who will rest well whatever may befall?
"Why care in what strange garb of horrors new
   " Is clothed the doom that waits us all?

" What if some fresh unfailing age of gold,
" Should fill each radiant galaxy with bloom?
" The man whose race is run, whose tale is told,
  " Owns nothing but his tomb.

" Thus whether Nature still uphold her powers,
" Or all things die at last, as men have died;
" Stop not to ask if that sure grave of ours
  " Be coffin-narrow, or world-wide."

We answer thus—The cloud before us spread
Stains with its shadow all that nursed our prime;
Hope is the world's best blood, which, chilled or shed,
  Palsies the heart of Time;

Your grim futurity we cannot bear,
It shakes us now, like earthquake tides inrolling,
Imagination has her own despair,
  And hears your distant death-bell tolling;

She droops even now beneath those evil dreams,
That like hearse-plumes, wind-swept, around her nod,
And shrinks from that lost universe, which seems
  To her the corpse of God.

Let her still therefore guard her lamp, and fling
Away the terror under which she cowers,
Trusting in trance to feel the touch of spring,
  And the young struggle of the flowers,

Trusting that when the days are full, some thought,
Some presence, may dawn round us by and by,
So that, as prophets and as bards have taught,
   We men may live, not die.

Then if that hope which science off has thrown,
Be but our nurse's lullaby and kiss,
If Nature round the edge her seeds have sown,
   Only to hide the near abyss;

If all her visioned flowers and fruits, that smile
And fade not, where the living water gleams,
Be but as desert phantoms which beguile,
   Mirrored on phantom streams;

Though none the promised amaranth may reap,
We yet accept the boon—believing still
That the great mother means us well—and sleep
   In faith, according to her will.

A FAREWELL.

TO HELEN.

Hadst thou been steadfast, I had made
    Thy name a seated star,
A Quenchless Beacon-fire, displayed
    To Times and Realms afar.

Hadst thou been steadfast! But thy heart,
    Weak against storm and shower,
When sunshine threatened but to part,
    Closed like a trembling flower.

Young flower, blush on, I blame thee not,
    Enrich the summer air,
And twine around another's lot
    Thy bloom and freshness rare.

Only the Immortal orbs of Heaven
    Faithful through darkness are,
Nor to the Earth-born rose is given
    The spirit of a star.

THE SECOND OLYMPIAN ODE OF PINDAR.

HARP-RULING hymns, What god? and then
   What hero claims our solemn songs?
Who also of the sons of men?
   First Pisa here to Jove belongs:
Next Hercules, who first this proud
Olympian festival endowed,
   With spoils from battle borne away;
Last Theron, whose four fiery steeds
   Have drawn a conquering car to-day,
Theron the Just, an honoured name,
Our choral anthems shall proclaim.
Of all his noble race the flower,
The pillar of his people's power,
   The helper of their needs.
After long toil and wasting woe,
   His fathers made a home their own;
Beside the sacred river's flow,
   The light of Sicily they shone,
And Fate, on their true spirits gently down,
Shed wealth unstinted, and unstained renown.
But, O great son of Rhea! Lord

Who deignest from thy heaven to guide
Our path through the Alphean ford,
　To these high rites, our country's pride;
Soothed by my strain, in love divine,
　The rich fields, which their fathers till,
　Through age on age, unchanging still,
To children yet unborn assign.

That which is past is past, just or unjust,
　Not Father Time himself, the root of all,
　An act once done can alter or recall;
Though, if kind heaven so will, oblivion's dust
　May cover it with darkness, like a pall.
For struggling evil dies, though late,
　By joyous pleasure crushed and slain,
When, out of sorrow, conquering fate
　Builds up proud blessedness again.
Cadmus, thy daughters sit at last,
　Each on her ever-during throne;
　Clear by their fate that truth is shown,
Through bitter agonies they passed,
But now, all gloom is scattered quite
By the strong sunshine of delight.
　High in Olympian splendour, one,
(She who to death was smitten, under
The roar of the unpitying thunder)
Thy long-haired Semele, to light restored,
Blooms on, by Pallas loved; by Jove adored,
　And by her ivy-crownèd son:

Yea, and to Ino, deep within the seas,
  The gods, our legends tell, have fixed to give
As Ocean Queen, sweet hours of golden ease,
  So long as Time shall live.

When man, frail man, to earth must go,
  No steadfast tokens mark;
Nay, day by day, we cannot know
If the swift daughter of the sun
Her happy course throughout shall run,
  Or tire before 'tis dark.
For with capricious interchange
  Of smiles and tears,
  Through life's wild years,
Must joy and sorrow ever range.
And thus the powers who govern still
  Each star which rules this ancient race,
  The god-given bliss at times deface,
And blast with some returning ill;
From that dark hour, when hurried on
By unrelenting fate, the son
His father Laius met and slew:
A deed which proved, with horror rife
  To all the shrinking tribes of man,
That the old Pythian voice was true;
This, when the avenging Fury knew,
She drained, in foul intestine strife,
  The blood of all that warlike clan;
Then Polynices died in shame;

Then, last leaf on the blasted tree
Of the renowned Adrastidæ,
   His child was left alone.
Thersander, in each youthful game,
And in the rush of war, a name
   To honour widely known;
Sprung from that root, all that our hallowing songs,
All that our harps can give, to Theron now belongs.
   For he on this Olympian plain
      The sacred crown of conquest wears;
   Whilst kindred wreaths, from Pythia's fane,
   And from the Isthmian Feast again,
   Urging four steeds that spurn the rein,
      His loved and only brother bears,
Whose triumph, as the hot wheels roll
Twelve times around that echoing goal,
   The just award declares;
Such victories, which men toil to gain,
Unbind the knotted brows of pain.

Wealth, if alive with virtue's golden light,
   Gives to deep love of honour strength and scope,
And opens wide to our uncertain sight
   The glorious avenues of golden hope.
Wealth is the vivid star which all may scan,
Shedding true lustre on the heart of man,
   If he who owns it will but feel within,
That coming hour, which comes to each,
When the strong hands of vengeance reach

Each lawless soul, that dies the slave of sin,
When each dark deed of treachery and blood,
Done in this corner of the world of God,
      Far under earth
      To second birth,
In penal horror rises once again,
Before some shadowy judge whom iron Fates constrain.

Then, then the good beneath a sun, whose light
Shines ever without setting day and night,
    A happy time begin;
By their worn hands the earth is vexed no more,
Nor the sea smitten by the toiling oar,
    A scanty meal to win.
To them in ever-blooming youth,
Among the heaven-loved sons of truth,
    That tearless œon rolls away,
Whilst others, whom we dare not glance at, groan
Through the long ages racked by pangs unknown,
    Until their bitter debt they pay.
But some there are, whose energies endure
    Thrice to recross death's gulf, and still
Through those three lives to keep the spirit pure
    From every taint of ill;
Jove leads these on, crowning their brave endeavour,
    To Saturn's home of happy rest,
Where the soft ocean breezes float for ever
    Around the island of the blest.
    There golden bloom to bloom succeeds,

With rays which never tire,
They sparkle on the ground below,
Out from the glancing trees they glow,
Their growth the very water feeds,
And burns a stream of fire.
Decked thence with those undying blooms, they shine
Girt with God's living light,
Where Rhadamanthus shapes the will divine,
To issues wise and right.
He, who with power and depth of counsel graced,
At Saturn's side, as fellow judge, is placed,
Saturn, by ancient fate the husband given
To Rhea, throned above them all in heaven:
Peleus and Cadmus flourish there,
And thither, from the Stygian shore,
When she had bent Jove's heart by prayer,
His mother great Achilles bore—
Achilles, whose wild wrath o'erthrew
Hector, the stubborn prop of Troy,
Who hand to hand proud Cycnus slew,
And bright Aurora's Æthiop boy.

Full many a shaft of song, till now unflown,
Deep in my heart, as in its quiver, lies;
Each shaft, when shot, has meaning for the wise,
But blindly dull, the mass of common mind
Must hope a fit interpreter to find.
The Bard is he whom nature calls her own,
And stamps all knowledge, as a whole,

THE SECOND OLYMPIAN ODE OF PINDAR. 299

    Upon his many-sided soul:
Whilst those who labour, night and day,
    To learn what none can teach,
Still meanly fluent, waste away
    In streams of idle speech;
Like jackdaws, shrieking envy as they rove
In terror round the bard divine of Jove.
    Oh, poet soul of mine,
Bend on the mark thy bow, once more proclaim,
At whom in love thy spirit glance shall aim
    The glory-giving shafts divine.
To Acragas, from eye in truth uplifted,
    My wingèd words they bear,
That, if a hundred years were searched and sifted,
    Theron beyond compare
Would stand her noblest son; If fruitful thought,
Or kindly heart, or generous hand be sought.
But envy, cherished in the foolish crowd,
    Still chattering on, must seek, in truth's despite,
O'er noble deeds to throw oblivion's cloud,
    And drag down honour to the common height.
Go, count each sand-grain on the storm-swept beach,
Then Theron's deeds of love let number reach.

THE FIRST CHORUS IN THE BACCHANALS.

FREE TRANSLATION.

From sacred Tmolus, and from Asian soil,
    Our dancing feet these plains have trod;
Pursuing evermore our pleasant toil
    In honour of the Bromian god;
Whilst our great lord with reverence due we greet,
Labour fatigues not, pain itself is sweet.

    Who keeps the path, the path we strike?
        Within the house who hear us,
    The first must flee, and both alike
        Breathe words well-omened near us;
Whilst I uplift the solemn chant divine,
Due to no other than this lord of mine.

    How blest is he, how blest is he,
        Who on the great gods leaning,
    Learns, in a life by them set free,
        Each secret's inner meaning;

His soul in mystic purity he steeps,
    And on the tottering mountain-heights,
With Bacchanals all raving round him, reaps
      The fruit of holiest rites.

Whilst the Great Mother's name, loud-bruited
    In frantic tumult onward sweeps,
Her wildest orgies, unpolluted,
    A law unto himself, he keeps;
Wreathed ivy trembles on his tossing curls,
The pine-crowned thyrsus round his head he whirls,
    And thus he speeds o'er land and sea,
    Oh mighty Bacchus! honouring thee.

Ye Bacchic nymphs, bear Bromius on,
    A god himself, of God the son,
From cliffs of Phrygia bear him down,
Through each wide-streeted Grecian town,
That stormy lord of vines, whom late,
Entangled in the nets of Fate
And racked by throes, beneath the blast
    And whirlwind of winged flashes,
From her dead womb his mother cast,
    Consumed herself to ashes;
Thus hapless she departed from this earth,
    Stretched ghastly in the lightning's glare,
But he was borne to a strange home of birth,
    By Saturn's royal heir.

Deep in the thigh of Jove immured,
    A thigh which golden clasps embrace,
From Juno's jealous hate secured,
    Our half-born deity they place;
Then when the Fates had ratified the time,
And decked his brow with branching rays sublime,
    O'er his wild votaries to reign,
    Our god perfected rose again;
With dragon wreaths his brow they bind,
    Wherewith his Mænads, in their play,
Coil over coil, a net-work wind,
        Around the struggling prey.

Thou, Thebes, which fostered tenderly
    The sun-bright youth of Semele,
        Your streets let clustering ivy strew,
        Pour floods down of bright-fruited yew:
        And rush to revelries divine,
        Under thick boughs of oak and pine.
Bind, bind your dapple fawn-skin raiment duly,
    With bands of fleecy wool, snow-white,
Shake, shake your staffs, to all cold laws unruly,
    But still fulfil each holy rite:
Soon the whole earth, stretched wide before us,
Shall reel beneath our rushing chorus.
Whilst Bromius leads from hill to hill,
    His dancers o'er the mountain land,
Where women crowds, awe-stricken still,
        To wait his coming stand:

Whirled far away, like leaves, from looms and
      spindles,
By the great spirit-storm our master kindles.
Ye haunts of Crete, with Godhead rife,
Where Zeus himself awoke to life,
Curetan cloisters, dimly spreading,
Which holy feet are ever treading;
Where, amid branching cavern glooms,
The Corybants, with triple plumes,
Roused from round drums of strainèd skin
    The storm of sound that slept within;
Then, in sweet interchange, they deftly blended
    That sullen roar with piping shrill
From Phrygian flutes, whose mellow breath ascended,
    Each solemn pause to soothe and fill.
    To honoured Rhea, in proud pleasure,
    Thence bore they that melodious treasure,
    A strain more fit than any other
      To mingle with our Bacchic shout;
    Therefore at once from the Great Mother
      Her satyrs rushed, a maniac rout,
To pour their doubling drum's tumultuous voices
Through those triennial feasts in which our god
      rejoices.

    His feet are joyous, when they strain
      Up to the mountain height;
    Nor do they tread the level plain
      With less delight.

He rushes on with frantic laugh,
    Clad in his sacred fawn-skin coat,
To rend the limbs, and fiercely quaff
    The life of slaughtered goat.
To eat in furious glee the flesh
    Of the yet writhing prey;
Whilst mountains, ever rising fresh,
Lydian or Phrygian, as may chance,
Like clouds, beneath our flying dance,
    Reel dizzily away.
'Tis Bromius leads the frantic rout,
'Tis Bromius raises high the shout;
Earth flows with milk, with wine it flows,
    It flows with nectar of the bee;
Whilst odorous mist around him throws
    An incense like the Syrian tree.
Hither and thither Bacchus turneth,
    From his pine-sceptre scattering fire,
Which, like a blood-red beacon, burneth
    To hearten those who stray or tire;
His words thrill madly through our throbbing pulses,
    His golden curls stream wide asunder,
Unceasing clamour heaven and earth convulses
      But still, through all,
      His proud words fall,
    And ride the subject storm in thunder.
Haste, haste, ye nymphs, bright-eyed, white-handed,
Fair flowers from Tmolus golden-sanded,

CHORUS FROM THE BACCHANALS.

Adore your Bromius, as he comes,
  With sea-like boom of groaning drums;
Let Phrygian yells in grim devotion,
  Let Phrygian pipes with tender chime;
  Let Phrygian pipes keep time, keep time,
To every strange and mazy motion.
Through which on mountains wild and lone,
Filled full of joys before unknown,
  And, driven by her unsparing god,
Like a young foal, light leaping round
Her mother, grazing o'er the ground,
    With eddying limbs,
    Each Mænad swims,
Amid the shriek of breathless hymns,
In her swift dance, whose whirling dims
    With wild amaze,
    The eyes that gaze,
And shakes the mountain sod.

THE TWO DESTINIES.

Over the swarming town, the moon
Looks through the fresh blue skies of June;
When, without rest, each fevered street
Throbs to hot wheels and hurrying feet;
When all contending passions pour
Their tides to swell the gathering roar,
And the great life-flood rising high,
Races in sparkling tumult by,
Close-shrouding underneath the gleam
And foam-flow of the upper stream,
Each sullen pain that lurks and creeps,
Dim-festering in its hideous deeps.
Yet, of the millions that it holds,
Whom some vague common name enfolds,
The working men, the mass, the poor,
Flowing through time, for evermore—
Like billows on a boundless sea,
Each noteless in immensity;
Not one, but moves through earth alone,
With a live spirit all his own,
And then, goes home to God on high—
A separate immortality.

Oh! there are hours when sickening thought
Deems the proud present dearly bought,
When all the mystic blessings given
Out of world-covering widths of Heaven—
All that man's work, since Nature's prime,
Has lifted from the gulfs of time,
Seem but as coloured meteors sent
Across a rayless firmament,
Which, ever as they brighten, wear
A blacker background of despair;
So that prophetic shudderings roll
Through the deep instincts of the soul,
As if, on wings divine outspread,
A curse were floating overhead.
Long-ripening growths of pomp and power,
Ere this, have withered in an hour;
Yea, on that eve, when, led by fate,
The Persian smote her brazen gate,
By false Euphrates watched no more,
And dashed her from her ancient place,
As white o'ersweeping waves efface
A footmark planted on the shore,
Clear like to-night, the moonbeam shone
High over doomèd Babylon.

Hark! to the merry music, wide
It breaks from yonder house of pride;
Where all that wealth can do, is done
To gild the minutes as they run.

Each window of the perfumed room,
Burns with keen splendour on the gloom;
The very air within it seems
To flash and thrill with gem-like gleams;
Whilst a mock nature spreads and showers
Voluptuous floods of breathing flowers;
And all things bright and soft combine,
As if man's lot were yet divine;
And never touch of sin or care,
Had power or thought to enter there.

Meanwhile around the stately gate
Throng creatures of a separate fate;
Hard-handed men, whose life alway
Is a sore wrestle with the day:
And dingy women, wrinkled deep,
Through schemes for bread and shorten'd sleep;
With no ungentle thought they come,
Each by a quenchless instinct led
From that gay place to carry home
Bright pictures to his gloomy bed:
By coarse unsmiling toil opprest,
They thirst for beauty and for rest;
And therefore, half unconscious why,
On each sweet face that passes by
They fix a pleased and grateful eye,
With no more envy than is given
To sunset clouds, or stars in Heaven.

At that proud door, distinct in all
The clear blaze streaming through the hall,
Met thus two girls, both young, both fair,
Far, far apart in all beside—
Fate for one moment brings them there
Together—then they sunder wide:
Yet this was witnessed by the heart,
Not vainly did they meet or part.
With undulating gleam, the first
Shot soft and sudden through the crowd,
As mellowest summer lightnings burst,
In gentle radiance, from their cloud;
The second, brightly pale and worn,
Drooped with meek face and hopeless eyes,
As, white and weak, a star at morn
Looks faintly into hostile skies.

One step—one look—ere it was done,
Each with her separate thought passed on—
Through all the music, mirth and light,
Through the sweet flatterings of the night,
The high-born maid, against her will,
By that sad face was haunted still;
And felt her joyous spirits wane
In dim disquietude of pain,
As half afraid, and half ashamed,
Over that lot she turned to brood,
And thoughts undreamt of and unnamed,
Like living things, before her stood—

Till vision-like, the glittering whole
About her seemed to swim and roll,
And a vague horror grasp'd her soul,
As if those void imaginings
Were memories faint of bygone things,
As if a dead past full of pain
Flamed up below her heart again
In fiery thoughts, which seemed to flow
Out of lives ended long ago,—
Her old lives through their trance within
Stirred by vague dreams of grief and sin,—
Hence through her stainless heaven of youth
(All child-like purity and truth),
Black phantoms of each former state
Streamed back—A shadow and a weight;
So that by instinct passing through
Whatever courteous speech was due,
She, on the shining masque around,
Gazed yet with wondering look profound,
Heard almost through the mirthful din,
A viewless summons trampling in,
And half prepared herself to go,
As if the life she seemed to know,
Were but a juggle and a show;
And she, when from the cheated brain
Ebbed off at length her visions vain,
In some foul den of gloom and shame,
Must wake,—Another and the same;

Meshed in the secret nets of fear
Thus throbbed the heart of Edith Vere.

As from the light she turned away,
Not such the thoughts of Ellen Gray :
To her no visioned griefs were sent,
No fancies stirred her as she went ;
Like a quenched fire, dust-choked, and blind,
Blackened the dreary past behind,
Before her, Life, without one ray,
In hard and icy clearness lay ;
She knew, from her own blasted youth,
What human hearts are born to bear,
And had been slowly taught, by truth,
The meaning of the word Despair ;
So that, when through the breezy night,
Like as to colour, age, and height,
In her young freshness of delight,
Edith swept by across her sight,
A strange emotion flitted o'er
Those pulses faint and low,
And her white face was flushed once more,
Yet not in envy. No ;
She shook her head and sadly smiled,
In pity on the radiant child,
That one so bright and sweetly frank,
Should know so little of her state,
As to have faith in life, and thank
The dull cold irony of fate,

Bent, in bad mirth, to make her think
She had no bitter cup to drink :
" Poor thing !" she sighed ; "so gay, so fair,
" How much for her to learn and bear !
" Trinkets and dress, the play, the ball—
" The Rest of Death is worth them all ; "
And a wild pleasure through her ran,
As the hard rending cough began.
Thus came together on that day,
Sweet Edith Vere and Ellen Gray.

How marvellous is man ?—how strange
The colours of his ceaseless change ;
. . . Kings, empires, creeds, are rolled away,
Faint scenes of a forgotten play :
Whilst that which seems thrown forth by chance,
The form, the hair, the brow, the glance,
Lives through the crush of ages, still
Unconquered and immutable :
Severing those alien creatures, though
Gulfs wide and deep as ocean flow,
Still rests on each young form and face
The beauty of their kindred race,
That mystic stream, whose fountain-head
Clouds of unfathomed eld o'erspread.
With heavenlike eyes, and golden hair,
After one type the damsels were,
Recalling eras dim, amid
The gloom of Saxon thickets hid,

When two such maids, of even birth,
Had trod with equal steps the earth.
Yes, far along the night of time,
We track the lovely of our clime;
Plunged in Hercynian forests hoar,
Among each grim Teutonic horde,
Such charms were honoured and adored,
Uncounted age on age, before
Our clear-eyed rovers of the north,
In their world-wasting ships went forth;
And even now, through all between,
So bright in these, that link is seen,
So rich and pure their common blood,
Against diluting years has stood,
That it is scarce too bold a dream
Of them, as spirit twins, to deem
That where through the vast halls of doom
God works apart in circling gloom.
And evermore by hands unknown
The dice of life and death are thrown;
Among the multitudes to be,
When touched and named by destiny,
The silent sea of souls that wait
For their earth-garments at the gate,
They, side by side, with necks of snow,
Bright locks, and eyes of azure glow,
From century to century,
Their white arms folded patiently,
Through immemorial time had stood,

Shadows of German womanhood.
And well might Ellen wish that Fate
Cycles ago had placed her there,
To smile on a barbarian mate,
With oak-leaves round her golden hair,
Against each fierce invading clan
To arm that stately hero-man,
To weave all day the robes of white
And purple that he loved to wear,
Then listen, breathless with delight,
To his returning tales at night—
"How he struck dead—no comrade there—
"Slow winding up the caverned lair,
"Among her cubs, the growling bear—
"Or, face to face, within the wood,
"Against the frantic Auroch stood,"
Hutted beneath some giant tree,
Where the bird sang, and boomed the bee,
With children ruddy at her knee;—
Or, earlier, in her virgin pride—
When kindred nations far and nigh
Met at some old solemnity,
And the grim gods, who ruled the wood,
Had drunk their fill of hostile blood—
Coming at perfumed eventide,
Under cathedralled branches dim,
To mingle in the dateless hymn,
Which through the echoing forest glades
Thrilled from a thousand fair-haired maids,

Whose glossy tresses tremble bright,
Whose eyes and teeth flash back the light,
Whose blue-veined arms shine rosy white,
Then mellow underneath the night,
As round and round, now swift, now slow,
Each in the undulating track
First gleaming out, then deepening back,
Their slight and graceful eddyings go
Past savage fires, wide-roaring through
Vast rifts of oak and roots of yew,
As still in wreathèd windings new
They time their virgin movements true,
Like some fresh river in its flow,
To their own voices sweet and low;
Whilst the green foliage overhead
Shoots into fits of glimmering red,
Each blood-like gush that comes and goes
Flung dark against the pale repose
Of moonlight openings through the wood,
Bathed in a breathless silver flood.

Yes, in primeval years, before
This world was rotten at its core—
Each natural gift, each inborn grace,
'Mid the far forests of the past,
Had blossomed in its destined place,
Lovely and fragrant to the last.
Thus had these two in Teuton hordes—
Whose history is the clash of swords—

Been sisters worshipped by the bold,
As were the German girls of old.
Two rosebuds, wild and sweet, would then
Had touched with joy the souls of men—
Now delicately nurtured, one
Drinks the sweet air, commands the sun,
Absorbs for ever, as of right,
The dew and freshness of delight,
Art-strengthened with unhoped-for powers,
Bursts into unimagined flowers,
And crowds some cool luxurious room
With clustered stars of burning bloom,
Whilst the poor sister floweret thrust
Beneath thick clouds of cankering dust,
Gnawn at the root by rat and snake,
Whose teeth infect the wounds they make,
And choked with charnel fogs, which break
Into foul splendours, but to fill
The air with venom deadlier still,
By faint instinctive struggling tries
To blossom into life—but dies,
And no one misses aught, or knows
The story of the blasted rose.

Alas, for Ellen Gray!—see where
On weary step she seeks her home,
No Saxon maid, with braided hair,
Along the bending woods to roam—
But a weak friendless girl, whose feet

Fall feebly on the echoing street,
As up the narrow lampless lane
She threads her way in patient pain,
To pant for hours, with fevered breath,
On her hard bed, and wish for death.

Alas, for Ellen Gray!—to her
Kind nature "seemed" to minister,
But all, that 'neath a happier star,
Had floated, like a glory spread
Around that young and radiant head,
A glory poured through space afar,
From spheres which shape all fates that are,
To the world's thrall, and victim, were
Sent as a mockery and a snare—
Delusions ending in despair!
The beauty which in Edith Vere
Was as the master-key to life,
Had been to Ellen, in her sphere,
A cup, with luscious poison rife—
The fresh hopes which for Edith Vere
Brightened the dusky wings of time,
To Ellen in her clouded prime,
Burnt like alluring cliff-fires, near
Ship-swallowing surf, on coasts of fear—
The softness which on Edith Vere
Waited, a magic shield and stay,
Became when leant upon, a spear
To pierce the heart of Ellen Gray.—

Surely when things like this befall,
Death cannot be the end of all?
All civilising arts we boast.
What does the vaunted progress cost?
Alas for earth, if this great gain
Have its foundations laid in pain—
Pain of the poor, who suffer still,
Let the world brighten as it will;
Nay, in the rough rude times of old,
When steel had lordship over gold,
Their life showed better hope and plan,
Stood straighter before God and man,
Groan'd less, smiled more, and, on the whole,
Sent into death a nobler soul.
Is this the end, then, which the wise
Have toil'd at through long centuries?
What are these poor? to pain consign'd—
Do they—or who, make up mankind?
Was it for others? or for them,
That Christ laid down His diadem?
This world has riddles hard and old—
Old as itself—not mine the power
Their inner meaning to unfold;
Still it is well, from hour to hour,
To keep them clear in view, and know
How blessedness contrasts with woe—
How some are ever breathing here
A bright and balmy atmosphere,
Whilst others, through unbroken gloom,

Unheeded falter to the tomb.
Therefore my story I resume,
And tell to all, who choose to hear,
Of Ellen Gray and Edith Vere—
How they were born, and lived, and died,
Earth's joy and sorrow side by side.

When, as a bright bird taking wing,
The south-west wind rose up in Spring—
And, like things bounding in a race,
Almond, and cherry-tree, and pear
Rushed into blossom everywhere;
Whilst up and down through Wyndcliffe Chase,
Wide-conquering hyacinths o'erthrew
The fresh green grass with floods of blue,
Till to the azure ground was given
The look of a reflected heaven—
Then, in a soft and clear May morn,
The daughter of Lord Vere was born;
Loud were the cheers round Wyndcliffe Hall,
Merry the bells from Wyndcliffe Tower,
And a deep breath of joy through all,
To greet the coming of the flower.
Out rolled the amber ale in seas
Through fifty shouting villages;
Upon each breeze-swept hill afar
Shook, the night through, a crimson star,
Round which to eager merriment
Loyal of heart the people went,

Whilst, full of rest, a mother smiled
Upon her long unhoped-for child ;—
Such was the welcome ready here
To meet on earth young Edith Vere.

Four months before, a babe as fair
Unclosed her blue eyes to the air
Where the great city's central roar
Rose, muffled by the frost fog hoar,
Through which the sun, like one in pain,
Fainted, a red receding stain,
Whilst blackening snow, and squalid sleet,
Dashed fiercely up the loaded street :
To lay in weakness on her bed,
A woman needed to earn bread,
Whose elder children uncontrolled,
From hunger cried, and shook with cold,
Whilst debts, like snakes, around them crept,
And that poor mother, faint and chill,
Under the ragged bed-clothes wept
To see her needles idle still ;
This was, into her home of clay,
The advent of poor Ellen Gray.

And how moved on her after youth?
We know, but will not feel,—in truth,
Because with hard and sinewy hand
Men bear great burthens up, and stand
Asking their kind for work, not ruth,

The comfortable heart disowns
Sorrow unvouched by tears or moans,
Contrives through pity to obtain
Fresh pleasure still, not wholesome pain,
And shuts light out, lest it create
Live pictures of the poor man's state,
To mar with scenes too harsh and rude,
The "luxury" of doing good.
Around the infant Edith gleams
A fairy land of golden dreams,
New joys at hand, ere old are gone,
The babe in perfect faith moves on ;
Her mother's blue and watchful eye
Hangs o'er her, like a loving sky ;
A budding fault, in forethought mild,
Is weeded from the unconscious child—
A happy instinct of the heart,
For ever fixed ere it depart—
Whilst to each gliding hour is brought
Some feeling new, or fruitful thought—
For one there was, who, day by day,
In grief or mirth, at task or play—
Like some great artist bending o'er
His work, which is to die no more—
As she o'erlooked, and viewed the whole,
Ever breathed in a living soul.
How, meanwhile, might poor Ellen fare?
Her childhood had no leave to wear
That golden gloss of infancy,

(Still, still above her hovering high
The shadow of grim want), she stood,
Forced from the first to do her best,
And join the strivings of the rest.
In the hard school of poverty,
She learnt the price of coal and wood,
And trusted to the roaring street,
In baby phrase, on tottering feet
Bargained and fought for bread to eat,
Time failed them to sow wholesome seed—
Time failed to watch her or to lead.

Thus mind and heart, of help bereft,
To nature and to chance were left;
Wild flower and weed, could come and go,
Virtue or vice, at will might grow;
Unchecked, unguided on its way
Went the young step of Ellen Gray.
As with their lot they struggled well,
Sickness on her brave father fell:
He bore, for months, pain's utmost force
In silence, as a thing of course,
Then worn by ceaseless toil and strife,
Died aged, in the prime of life,—
That lengthened illness swallowed all,
And when his spirit had found rest,
Want like a wolf, upon them pressed.
Then came from school the girl's recall,
The decent wish, that she should learn

Right ways, and perfect to discern;
The mother's pride, to hear her child
Praised as so docile and so mild,
Melted, like wax in flame, away
Before the hot need of the day.
When bread grew scarce and fires gleamed rare,
Her fingers were too deft to spare;
Some sorrow at the first there was,
Some hopeful talk, "The worst might pass;"
"Yes, next year better luck may bring;"
"She shall return there in the Spring;"
But Poverty kept near the door,
And, it was spoken of no more.

Thus on with Time they passed, and lo!
As from its bud a rose outbreaks,
The woman in the child awakes
To both alike, in fitful flow,
Swift blushes waver to and fro,
Warm looks of light gleam softly through
Those humid orbs of deepening blue,
Whilst the stirred pulses flock to fill
The trembling voice, grown sweeter still:
Edith sits musing in proud halls,
The book in vain her thought recalls,
From her slack hand the pencil falls,
The sounds of music sink, or stray
In dreamy melodies away;
As through her breast new feelings move,

Foreshadowing the dawn of love—
It came in peril and in power!
How was she armed to meet that hour?
Poor, poor indeed, as a defence
Her bright and gracious innocence—
No rampart round the heart! no dream,
That words are other than they seem!
A spirit credulous of good,
And youthful life along the blood!
However sweet, to watch her bend
Above some rosy child, with eyes
Where thought and holy instinct blend,
Whilst the bright creature in surprise,
To her close clasping arms ensnared,
With limpid glance, half pleased, half scared,
Such depths of tenderness to see,
Sits hush'd, though happy, on her knee—
However beautiful, to note
The vague delicious dreams that float,
Like warm mists of the golden South,
O'er her clear brow, and virgin mouth!
Well was it for that maiden fair
That she was placed, where none might dare
Slow schemes of hateful love to rear
Against the daughter of Lord Vere.
For her fear nothing, shielded warm
In her young bloom, she walks secure,
The very thought of sin or harm,
An exile from her spirit pure;

With faithful hearts to guide or aid,
Not safer as a child she played,
Her path with freshest flowers is strewn,
And, as she dances on her way,
Life opens like a rose in June—
Fear not for her, but Ellen Gray.
Alas, alas! what lies before
Cannot be spoken without tears,
Oh, that some loving hand of yore
Had slain her in her thoughtless years—
That her first sleep, with faltering breath,
Had dropped unbroken into death.

Poor child! no kind disease was sent,
No saving blow or accident—
Nought—such was mocking nature's will,
Stopped her from growing lovelier still;
Nor heat nor cold, nor days half fed,
Nor work in airless rooms by night,
Nor stinted sleep had power to shed
Over her budding youth a blight;
As to exhausting toil she went,
On her rich bloom long looks were bent;
Paid hags, with voices falsely sweet,
Beset her in the shadowy street;
Bewailed her labours long and sore,
Kept offering much, and promised more;
Teased her with visions of delight,
Pleasure all day, and rest at night;

But still she loved her mother, still,
Mixed with vague fears of shame and wrong,
A daughter's heart had kept her strong;
Her fancy wavered, but the will
Stood fixed all duties to fulfil;
And yet the evil seed was sown,
Vice wrestled with, not overthrown;
Her wild imagination flew
To the delusive light, that lies
Around hope's fleeting Paradise.
Daily her tasks more hateful grew,
More keen her thirst for something new;
More frequent the bewildered start,
Out from the beatings of her heart:
Still she bore up against it all,
Till her own virtues wrought her fall.
The mother whom she loved grew weak,
And suffered, though she did not speak;
Her earnings failed them; one by one,
The few coarse goods they owned were gone;
Those of a hard, yet happier, past,
And of the dead they loved, went last;
Until the dingy bed was all,
Between each black and tottering wall.
Vainly they called the Leech in aid,
Not harsh, but hurried, scarce he stayed,
Through that chill gloom, without remorse,
To speak these crushing words of course—
"There is no help in drugs of mine,

"She should have generous food and wine."
Yes, generous food and wine—from whom?
The breadless woman heard her doom,
And gazing, with one natural sigh,
On her lone girl, prepared to die;
But Ellen with suspended heart,
Trembled from head to foot apart.
She strove to pray, but all in vain,
Hot hands were clutching at her brain,
And swift sharp impulse on her course
Pressed her: A more than natural force.
With reeling step and face that burned
She went—hours past, and she returned,
Silent and white; then, dearly bought,
That generous food and wine she brought;
Some tale she told, "that she had seen
"Her clear soft eyes and gracious mien,"
Who with glad looks and gentle speech,
Goes round to comfort and to teach;
Whilst hope and sunshine up each lane,
Follow like handmaids in her train;
This soothed the first maternal fears,
And for long hours the sufferer slept,
Whilst from pale Ellen rolled slow tears,
As if a marble statue wept.
Time's lamp burns low as he grows old,
Clouds heaped on clouds our life enfold;
And for eternity we wait,
To light the gloomy depths of fate.

There silent Ellen weeps—and here
Thrills the sweet laugh of Edith Vere;
Whilst the rich woods round Wyndcliffe Hall,
Their leaflets to the breeze outfling,
Gemm'd with the showery gleams of spring.
Fresh pleasures, hopes unthought of, call
In flower-like loveliness arrayed,
With fragrance sweet the radiant maid;
Inheriting by right divine
The sovereign fiefs of beauty's line;
To wield the sceptre Heaven bestows
Over that spirit-realm, she goes.
On to her goal she moves serene,
As some bright ship, with placid motion,
Glides slow at first, enthroned a queen
Upon the sunny fields of ocean;
Then, when the waves rise up in play,
Pleased with the sparkle and the spray,
Drinks at each bound fresh draughts of glee,
And revels in the roughening sea.
Thus Edith sprung to meet the gale,
Spread out to hope her joyous sail,
Left calms behind, and found a home
Amid life's glittering drifts of foam.
As towered within her, hour by hour,
The sense of beauty and of power,
Her fancy kindled, and her mood
Ripened to perfect womanhood:
Too frank and guileless not to own

A rapture hitherto unknown,
When over all she felt from far,
Her presence rising like a star,
And even on the old and wise
New youth reflected from her eyes.
Each hint and motion of her will
The coldest hurried to fulfil,
Hung on her glances, to divine
The import of each look and sign,
Gazed with intensest yearnings, where
Passed the glad smile and golden hair,
And toiled in secret to produce
New pleasures for her honouring use;
Thus that gay girlhood in the sun,
A river of clear joy, rolled on.

A river of clear joy, on earth
But few such fountains now have birth!
How has devoted Ellen sped
At the dim pallet of the dead?
Yes, of the dead! That passive form
Is lent to darkness and the worm,
In spite of daintier food; in spite
Of soul-bought gold, flung forth to save,
God called her mother to the grave;
Near her faint groans, night after night,
Pale Ellen watched in wild affright,
Saw the dark truth with prescient mind
That idly struggled to be blind,

Seemed oft to feel the icy breath
Of deep, low whisperings from Death,
And heard his slow step creeping in,
Self-sacrificed (for what?) to sin.
Then came the end—and all alone
(Like sea-weed by the tide-mark strown),
She writhed unweeping on the floor,
To reckless desolation thrown,
Whilst without wants for evermore,
On slept the body, mute and cold,
For which her inner life she sold.
And lo! to fill its vacant place,
Vice without object, vain disgrace,
Heart-withering scorn, disease, despair,
Raised up by sneering fiends, stood there.
" Rise up, pale Ellen, time is brief;
" Not to the poor comes rest in grief—
" Rise, and go forth from this foul den,
" To haggle among hard-eyed men,
" With tightened brain and choking breath,
" About the dark details of death."
Soon with that dismal labouring,
Sounded the narrow chamber, where
She trembled on the single chair,
Whilst loud rough workers round it fling
Their rattling tools, and screw and plane
Scrape inwards on the aching brain.
Next from its tressels, night and day,
Glared the mean coffin—then came all

From which the wealthy shrink away,—
Last the neglected funeral.
Then first she wept, with sudden thrill
The heart relaxed its gates (until
The fountain of their flow was spent),
Beneath a storm of sorrow bent—
And when from this calamity
She lifted up her weary head,
And looked around—no friend was nigh,
The old dark room, the ragged bed,
Shared e'en from childhood with the dead,
Weighed on her quivering nerves like lead,
Whilst thoughts, that burned as fire, gave birth
To wild wrath against Heaven and Earth—
So she went reckless, and became
The inmate of a house of shame—
"Yes, Ellen, well may shudderings deep
"At that foul portal o'er thee creep:"
Common, nay vulgar, as all seems,
It is a home of evil dreams;
There broods around, above, within,
A cloud of immemorial sin,
Shrieks baffled at the sullen door,
Old bloodshed covered on the floor,
Whose ghastly essence, spread through all,
Peers like a spirit from the wall.
There fair young things, the prey of fate,
Attired in mournful finery wait,
And forth to careless vice are led;

All tremulous with ghostly dread—
No talk is theirs of ball or play,
Of glittering gems, or dresses gay,
Low whispering in their dreary room
Of the dim peoplers of the gloom—
How from the boundless vaults below,
Mysterious lights and moanings flow [1]—
How some are fated to behold
The soldier slaughtered there of old—
How stranger girls, lured in, then slain,
For double mercy scream in vain—
Bodiless voices thrill the air,
Footsteps unseen are on the stair,
Wild shadows waver, day by day
Draining the shattered heart away,
Whilst close about, within a call,
Thronged London's busiest murmurs fall,
And the black home of ghosts is rife
With all the ocean sound of life.

Soon these grim legends Ellen learnt,
Until her vivid fancy burnt
With a keen blaze, to madness near,
The fever of unceasing fear—
Locked in her narrow room apart,
With white dry mouth and hammering heart,
'Mid faces tumbling round she lay,

---

[1] These superstitions are not imaginary, but real.

And thirsted for the coming day.
Yet trembled when it came, lest there
Some grim look through the light should glare—
Whatever filled up time and thought,
No matter though a curse it brought—
Vice—degradation—insult—shame,
As respites from that withering dread,—
As a brief shelter from the dead—
All, all were welcome, all became
Points islanded in floods of flame—
Hence soon must whelming frenzy blind
Have overswept and quenched her mind,
But chance a timely exit gave,
And bore her from that living grave.

Star of the sullen universe!
Lone ray of ancient glory left
To smile on man, the heaven-bereft!
Sole conqueror of the primal curse,
Young love! there came a fire from thee
That set the captive trembler free.
Cheered by thy orb, a godlike force,
That frail girl's melancholy course,
Which pressed and pent, a buried river,
Sought sunless seas, to rest for ever,
In stifled wailings did not go,
One night-hidden, ice-caverned flow,
Beneath rock-rooted weights of snow;
If on its black breast, light divine

A moment gleamed, that light was thine.
Her beauty and her touching grace,
Which brightened even that hideous place,
Moved one to speak of love—the word
Fresh chords and maiden pulses stirred,
His wooings, hollow as they were,
She took—as smothered lights drink air,
And of her spirit young and sweet
Poured out the treasures at his feet:
Then, as from death-like insect sleeps,
A living flash, the fire-fly leaps—
Uprose she from those dungeon deeps.
Her lover stood, and smiled to see
The outburst of that burning glee,
By her heart fountains musing strayed,
To watch them as in flame they flamed,
Fed her on kindness, as you fling
Seed to a bird, that it may sing;
And made a study and a toy,
Of the deep passion of her joy:
But she, with full beatitude
Through her whole weary soul imbued,
Springs upwards like the lark in flight,
Drunk with the sunrise of delight,
The gloom behind, the cloud before,
Lie heavy on her heart no more,
Nor past, nor future are, amid
The present's luminous vapour hid:
The mere cessation of distress

Is unimagined happiness—
The comforts, common in our eyes,
Thrill *her* with rapture and surprise.
Long buried in foul streets, she goes
To greet the violet and the rose,
Rich lawns in blooming woods to grace,
And see great Nature, face to face;
In that new home, no words can tell
How joys on joys her bosom swell,
The everlasting youth of streams,
The blossoms tremulous with bees,
The grass shot through with wild-flower gleams,
The bright red kine among the trees:
Across the silence of her soul
In gusts of kindling music roll,
As on Æolian harps at night
The spirits of the air alight.
" Forecast not, pause not, tremble not—
" This is the wine cup of thy lot—
" Drink, Ellen, drink, whilst o'er it set
" The fiery freshness wrestles yet—
" Drink, Ellen, drink,—joy foams away,
" Night follows fast the golden day,
" This hour is thine—the next may shiver
" The chalice in thy grasp for ever."

As sweeps a silver cloud on high,
Across the pathway of the sun,
On Edith's dazzling destiny

The power of love his work begun :
The bright youth of her virgin brow
Pale shadows softening overflow,
Around each step, each look, each tone,
A veil of nameless grace is thrown,
And her blue laughing eyes, less bright,
Have deeper and more inward light.
Beautiful Edith! ever for thee
Life is not wholly ease and glee ;
Beautiful Edith! it is well,
Tears are God's gift, and this alone
Was wanting to complete the spell!
In sorrow, truth and worth are known,
Through its dark night with orbs divine
Stars of the soul arise and shine ;
The hard light of prosperity
Makes the heart fountainless and dry,
E'en thy rich nature, as it burst
Out with exulting bloom and growth,
Might have been withered down and curst
Into slow barrenness and drouth,
Of stream, and herb, and fruit bereft,
Nought but some mocking mirage left.

Only by what they here endure
Are men of their own hearts secure,
Through grief, howe'er with anguish fraught,
The knowledge of oneself is taught.
That which in joy is bud or flower.

Turns then to roots of living power;
So in thy lot, this chilling hour
On thy pure spirit set a seal,
And was for thee—as ice to steel.
Yes, Edith loved—no matter why,
Love yet is full of mystery,
Perchance between them viewless ties
And ante-natal sympathies
Caused it to be—perchance in heaven
Stars blended, unto whom was given
From skies that live beyond the sun,
A power to bind two hearts in one.
In both a sacred ardour burned,
Her deep love deeply was returned,
Nor was his heart, or form, or blood,
Unworthy of the maid he wooed—
But richer suitors soon drew near,
And kindly as he was, Lord Vere,
Of love, when weighed with rank and gold,
Thought in the temper of the old;
Then sorrowing hours dragged on their way,
Called by some solemn voice to bring
The night of thought—the feverish day,
With slow pale mists environing
The blighted promise of the spring.—
Then first she felt, in sad surprise,
The curse of alienated eyes;
And wandered like a homeless thing
Restless and faint in search of ease,

Through pleasures that now failed to please;
As if a river, in its flow,
Whilst summer lights around it glow,
Amid life's breathing warmth and flush,
Should find its waters cease to gush;
And a dim frost-breath o'er it run,
All else exulting in the sun;
So in bright scenes she stood apart,
With lonely coldness at her heart.

But she had learnt that not in vain
We strive with weariness and pain;
And soon her languid heart rose up,
Braced firmer by that bitter cup;
Tender and meek, but noble too,
Heaven left her worthy tasks to do;
Each opening morn an object brought,
And virgin dreams gave way to thought.
All fluttering fickleness above,
She made no compromise with love;
And yet passed on, star-eyed and straight,
With duty, through the narrow gate;
The moody silence of her sire,
Her lover's headlong fits of ire;
Ills great and small sunk down, subdued
By the pure beauty of her mood.
God gave her faith which nought could dim
In human spirits, and in him,
God gave her power to soothe and bless,

And the calm strength of gentleness;
Whilst aiding influences sweet
Out of the past like angels sprung,
Some glance that touched, some pulse that beat,
In memory's realm for ever young;
And heart-gifts sown in silence deep,
The Dower of Heaven and Time, scarce known
Until this fiery trial came on,
Pain-kindled now, as out of sleep,
To perfect form together leap;
So in the caves of Mother Earth
When some rich gas has travail-birth,
Its scattered elemental mould
Beneath compacting flame, is rolled
Into indissoluble strength,
And glows a deathless gem at length.

Yes, hearts, through consummating fire,
Ripened and nerved like gems, aspire;
But if too fierce and greedy heat
Long on the embryo diamond beat,
Its wrath to dregs and ashes may
Consume the sparkling seeds away;
Thus life dried up in Ellen Gray!
Ill-fated girl, she found her gleam
Of happiness a lying dream,
And the grim Future, kept at bay,
More ravenous soon, along her track
Roared in tumultuous hunger back;

Her weary lover put her by
In sated curiosity.
A broken plaything, a machine
Of which the wheels and springs are seen;
Such was she in his altered eye.
Day after day she saw aghast,
His languid kindness slackening fast;
Through the long night of sobs, and moans,
The raging fire of jealousy
Gnawed at the marrow of her bones;
Whene'er he left her, tears like rain
Fell till she saw his face again;
And oft through wet and snow-blast frore,
She tracked him from and to his door;
Dogging each step, that she might know
Where and to whom he used to go;
Enough, her charms, her love, were vain,
He left her, doubly now forlorn,
To curse the hour when she was born;
Full-sailed along a prosperous fate,
He left her without thought or care,
With breaking heart to alternate
From mad excitement to despair.
In that wild whirl out burst again
The half-quenched heat around her brain;
Her reason flickered—all but fled:
She knew not what she did or said;
Hither and thither would she go,
Racked with fierce merriment, as though

Into her veins had rushed a flood
Of fire, keeping time like blood;
Then for long spaces would she lie
Settled in black despondency;
And from herself strive hard to fly,
Trampling with reckless feet the mud
Of known and open infamy.
But this passed quickly; at the end
In nature's self she found a friend;
As the worn springs of life gave way,
She felt in gradual decay,
At length, from her world-wearied heart,
The fever and the flame depart—
Then softness came, and gentler woe,
Firm loathing of the hateful past—
Effort towards God's high will to go—
And yearnings to be pure at last.
Thus her health failed her, and anon
A burning thirst for death came on—
Oft in the living dreams of night,
Her mother kissed her, clothed in white—
Oft, crowned with stars, before her moved
The infant sister whom she loved—
Whilst low sweet voices seemed to say,
" Desolate creature, come away,
" Think of the words vouchsafed from heaven,
" Those who love much, have much forgiv'n,
" Thy sins, unselfish soul, shall grow
" Radiant as suns, and white as snow,

"Let thy prayers only be preferred
"To Him, according to whose word,
"Sounds yet among the sons of men,
"The name of Mary Magdalen;"
Thus, with life's leaf just on the fall,
Ellen saw Edith at the ball.
By her proud sire permitted now
Love duty-hidden to avow,
Thither, to meet the one most dear,
Went Edith, daughter of Lord Vere;
With smiles and glances archly coy,
After short sorrow, full of joy,
Yet though her smiles shone out once more
Her heart was other than before,
Past grief, pressed down by self-control,
Deepened the channels of her soul,
Not now a child, with reverent awe
The mystery dread of life she saw,
And felt a solemn instinct draw
Her spirit towards that crowd, for whom
There seems no shelter but the tomb;
So that pale Ellen's wasted form
Rushed on her like a summer storm,
And though they never met again,
Her memory kept the impress true
Of that faint step, and look of pain
Under gold curls and eyes of blue;
Hence many, whilst sweet Ellen lay
Released from all unhappiness,

Had cause, through after years to bless
The silent greeting of that day—
So true that witness in the heart,
" Not vainly do ye meet and part."
Happily now lived Edith Vere,
And Ellen's earthly end drew near,
Not comfortless, friends early known
Found her lost, homeless, and alone;
They had been harsh at first, and torn
Her spirit with their clamorous scorn;
Still be not sudden to condemn,
For character was bread to them,
To their dim hearths a tainted fame
Brought penury no less than shame—
Yet when she sunk beneath the load,
Their honest English hearts outflowed—
They lulled her pain, they soothed her mind,
Softly and delicately kind,
Till, praying with her latest breath,
She brightened gently into death.

A week passed on—half sad, half gay,
Blushed Edith on her wedding day;
The rites were done—with nought to sever,
She was her lover's own for ever—
Yet, duly given the parting kiss,
As she, to sure and growing bliss
Went in calm joy, each fiery horse
Was checked one moment in its course:

A parish coffin crossed her way—
Within it—slumbered Ellen Gray—
Bound for a calm and tearless shore,
The sorrow of a life was o'er:
There—wealth and love; here—death and rest;
None know but God which lot was best.

THE END.

Printed by R. & R. CLARK, *Edinburgh.*

www.ingramcontent.com/pod-product-compliance
Lightning Source LLC
Chambersburg PA
CBHW020325240426
43673CB00039B/920